A Universal Christian Faith

A Universal Christian Faith

formerly
"Catholic Quakerism"

Lewis Benson

The New Foundation Fellowship

First published in Gloucester, UK, 1966
Philadelphia Yearly Meeting edition:
First printing, July, 1968: 1,000
Second printing, August, 1973: 1,000
Third printing, November, 1977: 1,000
Fourth printing, June, 1983: 1,000
Fifth printing, January, 1990, 1,000.

New Edition, The New Foundation Fellowship, 2007

© Estate of Lewis Benson and The New Foundation Fellowship, 1966 and 2007

ISBN-13:
978-09519813-4-4

The New Foundation Fellowship
c/o Allistair Lomax, Brook Cottage, Chapel St, Fritchley, Derbyshire DE56 2FR

Typesetting and cover design by Peter Daniels Publisher Services

Contents

Acknowledgements vii

Preface to the Fourth Printing ix

Lewis Benson 1906-1986 xiv

Introduction xv

I. The Place of the Quakers in
   Christian History 1

II. The Quaker Understanding
    of Christian Ethics 20

III. The Quaker Conception of Christian
     Community and Church Order 37

IV. Catholic Quakerism and the
    Ecumenical Movement 52

V. The Recovery of the Quaker Vision 70

Appendix 86

References 90

Index 95

Acknowledgements

These five lectures were given at Woodbrooke, in Birmingham, England, during the autumn term of 1964. They would probably not have been written without the encouragement and stimulating criticism of Maurice A. Creasey, the Director of Studies at Woodbrooke. I wish to thank Maurice Creasey, and also to thank Arthur M. Windsor for preparing the index. I owe much to my wife, Sarah, for her many years of patient collaboration in the effort to bring to light the revolutionary character of the original Quaker message and mission.

Lewis Benson
Brielle, N.J., 1968

Editors' note, 2007

We are presenting this reprint of *Catholic Quakerism* by Lewis Benson because we think that the author's basic insights have lost none of their value in the intervening half century. Inevitably however some of the immediate circumstances have changed. Although we agree with the warning of Lewis Benson against a particular form of ecumenical engagement with the Protestant churches, the ecumenical process has developed in other ways, and in some places, that are not inconsistent with the stand taken by Lewis Benson. This has caused us to add an occasional footnote. We have not changed the original wording but we have omitted one or two phrases and statements that are not relevant or can no longer be understood. The essential message that Quakers are entrusted with a distinctive and universal (i.e. "catholic") understanding and practice of the Christian gospel is not affected.

Preface to the Fourth Printing

These five lectures were printed privately in England in 1966. In 1968 they were published by the Book and Publications Committee of Philadelphia Yearly Meeting, and reprinted in 1973 and 1977. On the occasion of the fourth American printing I am glad for the opportunity to take account of some changes in the historical situation and to say something about the way George Fox's revolutionary gospel message has spread since 1964.

When these lectures were first given, it seemed that there was a need to deal at length with the challenge of the ecumenical movement. The momentum of that movement has slackened with the passage of time, and fewer people are now dreaming the ecumenical dream. What I called "the hidden presuppositions" of the ecumenical movement (p. 69) have now come into the open, as is apparent in the recently adapted resolution that defines the World Council of Churches as "a eucharistic fellowship". The high purpose set forth at the Third Conference on Faith and Order, at Lund, in 1952, to "study Christ and the relation of Christ to his church and draw the consequences for the doctrine of the church," has been rendered ineffective by the intransigence of hard-core dogmatic orthodoxy.*

On the other hand, the Quaker society has tended to become more denomination-minded as it has been drawn into ecumenical relationships on several levels of cooperation. There are still Quakers who see a future in which the Society of Friends will find a place within some kind of ecumenical framework.

---

* A more positive statement of the true ecumenical spirit will be found on page 59: "To study Christ and let Christ order his church, and to lead people to Christ and bring them together in his body, the church, is a program in which all Christians can participate. *Solus Christus* (Christ alone) can be the word that binds all together and heals all wounds."

This may be largely due to lack of any other vision for the Society's future.

What most needs to be reported here is that these five lectures have not been seed that fell on barren ground. There is a growing number of people who have caught the "Catholic Quaker" vision and, since 1974, some of these have found fellowship in the task of reproclaiming the everlasting gospel that Fox preached.

Looking back with the wisdom of hindsight, I would say that the greatest weakness of *Catholic Quakerism* is that it is not specific enough about the gospel that Fox preached. This may not be just an error of omission. Since 1964 my understanding of the nature and content of this "everlasting gospel" has deepened.

In 1973 I received a clear call to go forth and preach this gospel. This call was accompanied by the proviso that I was not to speak of anything which I could not attest from my own experience. In 1974, working closely with Joseph Pickvance, I found myself scheduled to speak at five weekend gatherings in England on "What Did George Fox Teach about Christ?" In collaboration with John Curtis, we began to hold similar gatherings in America. I had never done anything like this before, and that first year was an adventure of faith. I had no choice but to concentrate as never before on the actual content of the gospel message that Fox preached. During this period I was often reminded of the saying that "There is nothing that so effectively improves the clarity of a man's thinking as to know that he is to be hanged in a fortnight." In this work we learn by doing.

I didn't foresee in 1974 that I would be making three more trips to England and that others would be recruited for this work, so that the everlasting gospel would be preached again throughout the U.S., Canada, and Britain, as well as in Japan, Ireland, France, and Spain. There is now a band of men and women (English, Irish, American, Canadian) belonging to fourteen different Quaker Yearly Meetings, who are engaged in this work.

The "work" is simply the task of reproclaiming the good news that "Christ has come to teach his people himself." These eight words are a kind of summary of the gospel that Fox preached at

Preface

Firbank Fell, the gospel by which he and his co-workers were able to gather about sixty thousand people to Christ in the seventeenth century.

This gospel message is a proclamation that Jesus Christ is alive and that he is in the midst of all who gather together in his name. But the *heart of this message* is that the living Christ is present in the midst of his people *in a functional way*. We can know him by personal encounter as he comes to us as our living teacher and leader, and as the living prophet, priest, and king of God's people. These functional roles are what Fox calls "the offices of Christ," and in both his accounts of his Firbank Fell sermon he makes his teaching about the offices of Christ the central feature of his message.

Some Christian traditions regard Jesus Christ as savior only because he has the power to forgive and pardon in his office as priest. But Fox taught that Christ is also our savior as he is our living teacher and prophet who teaches us what is right and gives us the grace and strength to do the right.

In preaching this gospel at weekend gatherings I have begun with the everlasting gospel that Fox preached. At later sessions, I have tried to show that this gospel is the foundation for new moral certainty and strength, both for the individual and for the fellowship of disciples, and that it is also the foundation for a new kind of church order with a new kind of worship and ministry. I have never failed to read at least a portion of George Fox's two accounts of his sermon on Firbank Fell at these gatherings.*

Since 1974 a growing number of workers has taken Fox's gospel message to hundreds of weekend gatherings, forums, workshops, and various conference opportunities. The need for longer residential opportunities under our own auspices has been partially met by summer gatherings in the U.S., Canada, England, and Ireland. At the first of these, at Haverford College in 1976, I gave five talks on "A New Foundation to Build On," and about this time the band of workers began to call themselves the "New Foundation Fellowship." What began in 1974 as the *Weekenders Newsletter* became the *New Foundation Newsletter*, published annually and *New Foundation Papers* appears four times a

*See Appendix

year. Both are published simultaneously in the UK and the United States.

The effort to re-proclaim the everlasting gospel that Fox preached has been essentially a grassroots operation. There are now New Foundation workers who are affiliated with evangelical, liberal, and radical liberal Yearly Meetings of Friends, and their work has carried them to a wide range of groups within the Quaker spectrum. In 1688 Stephen Crisp wrote, "Love all men, and labor for the good of all men," and every issue of *New Foundation Papers* bears on its masthead the declaration: "We seek the good of all."

In the seventeenth century Francis Howgill and Edward Burrough were the Quaker team who undertook to bring the everlasting gospel to London. In writing to them Fox said, "Stir abroad while the door is open." So many doors are open to this message today that it is difficult to find enough workers to match the opportunities. Fox also wrote to Howgill and Burrough, "Sow not sparingly." This New Foundation work has been international from the beginning and an effort has been made to go wherever the door is open. New Foundation workers are young and old, men and women, and they come from a wide variety of Quaker (and other) backgrounds. The New Foundation Fellowship is a task-centered group and its task is to lead people to Christ and to settle and establish them upon Christ, who is the "way to God, the head of the church, the rock and foundation that stands sure" (Fox, Epistle 368).

The "new" foundation that we are telling people about is new only in the sense that it comes freshly to present-day hearers in a challenging way. But it is as old as the gospel that was preached by the apostles, and by the Valiant Sixty in the seventeenth century. This gospel message is the heritage of all who bear the name of "Friends," but it has not been retained as a part of any living Quaker tradition.

Early Quakerism was what Dean Freiday has called "begin-again Christianity." We don't have to embalm the Quaker cause in a plurality of nineteenth-century traditions—evangelical, liberal,

---

* *The Friend* (London), Nov 9, 1979, p.1381.

Preface

or conservative. In the words of Ursula Windsor, "We can begin at a fresh point"*. Friends of several traditions are now doing this and finding a wonderful sense of fellowship in proclaiming Christ the one foundation, and in building on that foundation.

Three centuries ago the new Quaker apostolate went forth to preach the everlasting gospel. Their message evoked in their hearers a burning desire to gather in Jesus' name, to wait to feel his presence in their midst as their living teacher, prophet, priest, and king. As this same message is being preached today, it is causing those who receive it to know Jesus in a personal encounter as they meet together to feel his presence in all his offices.

In North America the New Foundation work is bringing something new to the Quaker scene. It has been good news to many Friends that they don't have to choose any of the current Quaker traditions and that they are not compelled to accept the dogma that Quakerism is, by definition, pluralistic. In Great Britain the preaching of the everlasting gospel has opened up new vistas. At the conclusion of one of our London weekends, one Friend was heard to say, "I always knew there was more to Quakerism than they have been telling us." Renewed interest in Fox's message has brought to light his teaching concerning Christian ministry, and this has focused attention on the all-but-forgotten story of the Quaker ministers and their ministry. In her article, "Quaker Ministry as a Vocation," Ursula Windsor has written with enthusiasm about this important part of our heritage.*

In the last chapter of this book I observed that for the Catholic Quaker vision "this is the winter season." I see signs everywhere that the thaw has now begun and we are approaching, if not summer, then at least early spring.

Lewis Benson

The Greenleaf

Moorestown,

N.J., 1983

---

* *New Foundation Papers* No. 8, April, 1982

Lewis Benson
1906-1986

Lewis Benson was a lifelong member of the Religious Society of Friends (Quakers). By profession he was a printer. Also, he was secretary of the Evanston, Illinois, Friends Meeting 1938-1942. But such activities did not prevent his study of George Fox and original Quakerism. His major concern was to find the source of the extraordinary life and power exhibited by the first Quakers in the 17th century. To do this he spent most of his life studying the writings of George Fox, the founder of the Quakers. He had a wide interest in Christian theology and social concerns. His personal library of over 1000 volumes is being preserved as a resource for scholars.

He was very tender towards seekers for truth and his letters were a help to many. *Catholic Quakerism* [now *A Universal Christian Faith*] is based on Lewis Benson's research and experience of original Quakerism and is a result of his concern that the message and experience of original Quakerism may be a help to everyone.

JOHN H. CURTIS

Crosslands
Kennett Square, Pennsylvania, 1989

Introduction

This book certainly changed my life. I have never been the same since meeting Lewis Benson. It was very unnerving. In a time of complete relativism, his surety of faith and purpose was alarming. Fortunately Lewis also had a great sense of humor. In his study was the picture of a man, living in a desert setting, checking his mailbox and opening a letter. The caption read, "Congratulations, you have been nominated for Who's Who on the Lone Prairie." I remember John Curtis telling the story of the time that Lewis first came to Evanston Meeting (IL) as the newly appointed Meeting Secretary. Evanston Meeting was a deeply divided group, a product of a recent merger of programmed and unprogrammed Quakerism. Lewis did not weigh in on the Liberal vs. Evangelical chasm at Evanston. Instead, he tried to present a new and different vision of Quakerism that was a challenge to both sides. This instantly united the Meeting—everyone against Lewis!

It took a lot of work but eventually John Curtis, Weldon Reynolds, and others began to see that there was something to what Lewis was saying. He really did understand George Fox's message. Lewis' view of early Friends was backed by his extensive scholarship on George Fox (see Benson Papers 1162, Haverford College Quaker Collection, Haverford, PA). Even more importantly, it was supported by his own very real experience of despair and transformation (see preface to the Fourth Printing). He knew that the Power of God, experienced by early Friends was not limited to their time for he had an encounter with this same Power in his own life.

Even with this progress at Evanston, Lewis remained an outsider. His extensive scholarship on Fox was often ignored because of his limited formal education. In a poignant and supportive review of *Catholic Quakerism* (*Friends Journal,* October 1966) R.W. Tucker wrote, "Benson's most conspicuous trait is his

Introduction

talent for making Friends extremely angry at him, he has been provoking hostility for years..."

Lewis had mellowed some by the time I met him in 1980. I was impressed by his humility, his sense of humor, and his ability to listen so deeply to the questions and concerns of others. He was at this point finding a real hearing among younger people who had become disillusioned with whatever brand of Quakerism they had tried. Time was already confirming much of what Benson had written in these pages. The latest Quaker idols were showing cracks and signs of decay and the slogan of "Unity in Diversity" were producing neither. People were beginning to listen to the timeless message of faith spoken and written about for so long by Lewis.

Why is this book (Benson's only full length writing) still so important to us today? Is it simply a Quaker Classic, to be assigned as required reading in a survey course? There is more, a great deal more to this book than simply presenting one side of the story. Within these pages is a contemporary message of Hope, Light, and Life. It can transform our world if we allow ourselves to listen beyond the words, to the substance of the message. This book is not simply about dismantling the idols of Modern Quakerism. It is a call to us to come out of the old into the new. Deep within the premise of this writing is the hope that we too can find this same living Word very much alive within us and among us, teaching us how to respond to our crumbling world.

Christopher Stern,

Philadelphia, 2007

Chapter I

The Place of the Quakers in Christian History

In this age of ecumenical conversation each participating denomination feels the need to try to find its place in Christian history. For some denominations the task of finding a satisfactory historical category presents no great problem. But church historians do not find the Quakers easy to classify. The Quakers themselves are not much help because they favor several differing theories and do not seem to be moving toward general agreement.

I will not attempt to examine all the various theories that have been employed to explain where the Quakers belong in the history of Christianity. Instead, I will survey some contemporary Quaker views, and then I will attempt to state the case for the view that Quakerism constitutes a comprehensive interpretation of Christianity which is catholic* in its conception.

In the Society of Friends at the present time there appear to be four main lines of interpretation leading to four different views of the place of the Quakers in history.

Mystical Quakerism

According to one of these views Quakerism is one of many outcroppings of mystical religion that have occurred from time to time in Christian history. In support of this view an attempt has been made to trace the spiritual ancestry of the Quakers through a long chain of Christian mystics. The Quakers are represented as one of the links in this chain.

*Note that Lewis is using the word "catholic" in its proper and original sense of "universal—that which is addressed to all men and women everywhere and seeks to include everyone."

Chapter I

Mystical Quakerism claims to be a recovery of the spirit and purpose of the original Quaker movement, but this claim has substance only in so far as its major premise is accepted. It asks us to start with the premise that the early Quaker teaching about the *light* can and should be understood in terms of Christian Platonism. This means that the term *light* should be understood as signifying the spiritual potentiality in human life, and that it refers to that part of man's nature which has kinship with the divine. As this premise became widely accepted the term *inner light* became the most commonly used expression for the central principle of the Quakers, and this *inner light* came to be associated more and more with man's highest spiritual potential and less and less with the unique savior, Jesus Christ.

Christian Platonism is a comprehensive system of religion that contains its own distinctive view of God, creation, history, man, sin and salvation. When Christian Platonism began to dominate the intellectual life of large sections of the Society of Friends it led to vast changes in Quaker life. The character of worship and ministry was transformed. Corporate witnessing, church discipline, the nature of Christian fellowship were seen in a new light and underwent radical changes. But it is not necessary here to dissect this Quaker version of Christian Platonism and examine each part, nor is this the place for a detailed study of the way in which the Quaker community was transformed under its influence. I wish to focus attention on the fact that as Quakers began to regard their faith as a form of Christian Platonism, this modified their view of the place of the Society in the history of Christianity.

When Christian Platonism takes root in a Christian society it does not transform it overnight. But it does transform it bit by bit and in the end it transforms it completely. At first it appears to change nothing in the life and structure of the society but only professes to offer a more rational and reasonable framework for religious thought. But mysticism is a phenomenon that is not peculiar to any particular historical religion. Each major religion has its own version of mysticism and although each version has its own distinguishing marks there is an unmistakable family resemblance that links them all. Christian Platonism is the classical form in which mysticism has appeared in Christian history and it is to the tradition of Christian Platonism that the mystics of other faiths turn when they seek for that form of Christianity that is most akin to their own religious interests and experience.

It is therefore not surprising that Quakers of the mystical type should begin to think of their faith as the Christian version of mystical religion and to claim a spiritual kinship with mystics belonging to non-Christian traditions. In fact, some Friends maintain that the special historical task of the Quakers is to be that Christian denomination that embodies the spirit of Christian mysticism and thereby serves as a bridge between Christianity and the mystical element in other religions. If the Quakers are, in fact, a denomination with this special calling, it certainly puts them in a special category and sets them apart from nearly all the Protestant and Catholic forms of Christianity.

For the Friends who have extracted these implications from the mystical interpretation of Quakerism it appears that Quakerism is neither a Protestant denomination nor does it belong to the Roman tradition but it constitutes a third form of Christianity, and it follows that in all inter-faith and interdenominational relations the Quakers ought to accept the role of spokesmen for this third form of Christianity.

There is a universalism that belongs to mystical Quakerism but it is not the universalism of the Christian faith. It is the universalism of mysticism. For the mystic, Christianity is one particular manifestation in history of an "eternal gospel" whose truth is not dependent on any historical events. To the question "Is Quakerism for everybody?" the Quaker mystic must add "Is Christianity for everybody?" To both questions he is compelled to give a negative answer. The truth as the mystic sees it cannot be limited to any one of the great historical religions.

Liberal Quakerism

Liberal Quakerism is another type of Quakerism that has come into prominence in the 20th century. It is a way of interpreting the liberty that was a part of the early Quaker vision. Quakers have avoided the use of formal creeds as a test of membership and they have been opposed to church discipline based on

Chapter I

church law and enforced by human authority. For the Quaker Liberal these aspects of Quaker life are primarily valued because they appear to give latitude for free ranging intellectual speculation. Among the Quakers the intellectual feels he has elbow room. The intellectual who is also an individualist is often unhappy in most Protestant denominations. He thinks of the Quakers as a form of Christianity from which creedal orthodoxy and priestly authority have been eliminated. And why should they have been eliminated if not to provide a spiritual home for such people as himself? The Quaker Liberal seldom goes much deeper than this in his understanding of Quakerism. To the Quaker Liberal, Quakerism means freedom to roam all over the religious map, and he values his liberty to do this and enjoys observing his fellow Quakers roaming freely about, even though they may be moving in directions very different from the direction in which he is moving himself. For many such the Society is primarily a refuge for those who want freedom to follow their own individual bent in an atmosphere that is mildly religious and fiercely tolerant. They see the Society of Friends as one of the liberal denominations and they feel a certain kinship with other liberal denominations.

The Liberal Quaker considers that the Society of Friends, like other liberal denominations, is small because it is appealing to a comparatively rare type of person, and he accepts this smallness as something that is inevitable and right. Although a liberal may hold almost any theological position it is very rarely that his position could be called evangelical. To be evangelical means to know one's group as having a truth committed to it that is for all men to share. The evangelical spirit is the antithesis of Quakerism as the Liberal Quaker understands it, and this spirit would destroy everything that the Liberal values in Quakerism.

The Liberal does not give much thought to the place of the Quakers in Christian history but he considers such a liberal sect as he conceives the Society of Friends to be as something that deserves to be maintained and perpetuated, and he is willing to work hard to keep it going.

Evangelical Quakerism

The third type of Quakerism is that which is called Evangelical. Evangelical Quakerism reached its high water mark in the second half of the 19th century. It appeared at a time when the Society had become greatly reduced in numbers under the influence of Quietism. Quietist Quakerism produced no means of propagating itself and during its long period of domination it removed many from membership through disownment. By means of the Evangelical movement the numerical decline was checked and new work was opened up in what was then called the "foreign mission field." There can be no doubt that at least half of the Quakers in the world today are the direct or indirect result of the activities of Evangelical Friends.

It is understandable that Evangelical Friends associated the term Quakerism with the bad old days of Quietist domination. They liked to say that it was "Christianity and not Quakerism" that they were concerned about. But of course by Christianity they meant Evangelical Protestant Christianity and by Quakerism they meant Quietist Quakerism. The distinctive features of the Society of Friends such as the free ministry, church government, corporate testimonies, etc., were regarded as denominational peculiarities which are secondary religious characteristics and which are not essential to the functioning of the Quaker denomination as an Evangelical Christian body. All of the distinguishing marks of a Quaker community have been abrogated by the various groups of Evangelicals at some time or other. For them, this is the unimportant side of Quakerism. What is important is Evangelical faith and experience as it is understood in the Evangelical Protestant tradition. This tradition is the home of Revivalism and Pietism and has an overall theological pattern that can be traced partly to Calvin and partly to Wesley but owes little to the Quakers.

This kind of Quakerism is by no means dead.* It still exists in strength in the western parts of the United States. The Evangelical Friends have never accepted either the liberal or

---

*At this point Lewis spoke of a "golden age" of Quaker Evangelicalism in the 19th century but we must not underestimate its present vitality and its spread into Latin America, Africa and Asia, and those countries where most Quakers now live.

mystical interpretation of Quakerism and have regarded them as tending to weaken the Christian foundations of Quakerism. Evangelical Friends believe that their role in Quaker history is to keep alive a Christ-centered Quakerism in an age when the Christian content of Quakerism seems to be fading away. They conceive of their role in Christian history to consist in being loyal to the Evangelical spirit and in leading the Society of Friends into an alliance with other Evangelical denominations and they are already actively involved in such an association. The members of this association are wary of the consequences of a too close participation in ecumenical activities because some of the larger denominations that are most active in ecumenical work do not measure up to their standard of Evangelical Christianity.

In recent years some attempt has been made by the Evangelical Quakers to study George Fox and the early Quakers. They have been happily surprised to find that Quakerism in its inception was Christ-centered and that it could certainly be called evangelical (with a small "e"). They seem to be largely blind to those elements in early Quakerism that are not found in their own tradition and so they find it easy to jump to the conclusion that their own Evangelical Quakerism is the only living tradition that is a continuation of what the early Friends started. They believe that the Evangelical Protestant denomination represents the truest form of Christian community and that Fox and the early Friends were among the pioneers who started such denominations. They therefore think of the true Society of Friends as a Protestant denomination of the Evangelical type.

A Fourth Point Of View

Since World War II a fourth point of view has made its appearance and seems to be gaining ground. It would not be easy to give it a name, but it can safely be asserted that it owes its beginning to dissatisfaction with the mystical interpretation of Quakerism. The exponents of mystical Quakerism had known all along that the evidence that early Friends were directly influenced by mysticism was inconclusive, and the best scholars were guarded in their statements and never tried to press this point. It was not necessary to claim direct influence if it could be shown that Quaker thought and experience were essentially mystical in character. The apologists for mystical Quakerism felt secure in the belief that they had established, once for all, that Quakerism is a species of mysticism. But as scholars began to take another look at the sources, some became convinced that we are not compelled by the evidence to give Quakerism a mystical interpretation.

The Quakers appeared in England at a time of great social and religious upheaval in which Puritanism came to be the dominant religious force in the nation for a time. It would have been strange indeed for the Quakers to have come into existence at this particular time without showing any signs of the influence of Puritanism or without having some of the characteristics of some of the separated Puritan groups. Some historians, like S. R. Gardiner, have not hesitated to call Fox's doctrines "the quintessence of Puritan protest against external formality."[1] However, not all church historians are willing to put Quakerism in the Puritan category unequivocally. Horton Davies says, "The Society of Friends, though technically not one of the Free Churches, has very close affinities with them."[2] Dillenberger and Welch call the Quakers "the most distinctive of the movements related to Puritanism."[3]

Geoffrey F. Nuttall, in his book *The Holy Spirit in Puritan Faith and Experience*, says of the Quakers that "in the exclusive sense [they] are not Puritans but the Puritans' fiercest foes" and he cites Thomas Taylor's statement that two years after Fox came to Westmorland: "many of those called Puritans was convinced." But he further states that the Quakers "repeat, extend and fuse so much of what is held by the radical, Separatist party within Puritanism, that they cannot be denied the name..."[4] He sees Presbyterianism as representing the oldest and most conservative party in Puritanism and Quakerism as the youngest and most radical.[5]

Geoffrey Nuttall's views have found wide acceptance especially among those Friends who have been dreaming the ecumenical dream. If the ecumenical movement is a movement out of disunity and into unity, then it is important for all the denominations who are concerned in it to understand the way their founders contributed to the disunity. Knowledge about how the disunity started may point the way to ending it. As we have seen, the Mystical, Liberal and Evangelical types of contemporary Quakerism do not come naturally into the orbit of ecumenical thinking. But if the Quakers were a Puritan sect and moreover, the "most radical" of the Puritan sects, then we have an historical relationship to Protestant Christianity which is comparatively easy to grasp. If the Quakers were the most radical among the Radicals then the questions will naturally arise, "Were they too radical?" and "In what way were they too radical?" Since the Quaker principle and practice with regard to the so-called sacraments (water, bread and wine) present a difficulty for the Quakers in most ecumenical encounters, the question has been raised as to whether this centuries-old Quaker testimony is an instance of carrying the Puritan protest against external formality a bit too far.

The Quakers are sometimes classified as one of those groups who, like the Puritans, have given the doctrine of the Holy Spirit a position of central importance in their faith and teaching. Geoffrey Nuttall suggests that there are some who hold that Quakerism's fresh perception of the implications of the doctrine of the Holy Spirit makes it representative of true Puritanism.[6] And Horton Davies states categorically that "The distinction of Fox and his followers was that they rediscovered the practical implications of the Christian doctrine of the Holy Spirit."[7] He believes that the phrase *Inner Light* is simply the Quaker term for the Holy Spirit.

The facts of history do not compel us to accept the view that the distinctive feature of early Quakerism is its doctrine of the Holy Spirit. This is not to say that early Quakers had no doctrine of the Holy Spirit or that this doctrine was not an important and integral part of their conception of Christianity. But it is *not* this doctrine which stands out as the chief feature of Quakerism and makes it easy to classify as a type of Christianity that makes this doctrine centrally important.

"The light that lighteth every man that cometh into the world" has been rightly called the Quaker's text but Fox does not usually identify this light with the Holy Spirit, whereas he does repeatedly identify it with Christ who rose again and sits on the right hand of God,[8] who is God's covenant of light,[9] and the heavenly prophet foretold by Moses.[10]

As we shall presently see, the central feature of Quakerism was its proclamation about Christ, the New Way to God, the New Covenant of Light, the head of the church, and the teacher of God's people. It is entirely legitimate to point out certain features of early Quakerism that were probably due to Puritan influence. But unless it can be shown that Quakerism follows Puritanism in its chief features and general pattern we cannot go on to assert that Quakerism is a species of Puritanism. Quakerism differed radically from Puritanism in its view of the scriptures, its conception of the nature of the church, its doctrine of Christian worship and ministry, its view of the sacraments, its belief in the moral perfectibility of both the individual and the church by the power of Christ, its view of the relation of the Christian to the state, and its understanding of the meaning of the cross. Quakerism was militantly engaged in an attack on Puritanism on all these points. This conflict was not an instance of the proclivity of sectarian Christianity to make a mighty controversy out of minor points of doctrinal difference. These were major points of difference and for the Quakers the controversy was seen as a struggle between two opposing conceptions of Christianity.

By whatever name this fourth trend in Quakerism comes to be known we can be sure that it is not by this path that the Quakers will recover their sense of universal mission.

Those who regard Quakerism as a species of Puritanism seem to feel that there is a "main stream" or "main current" of Christian tradition and the Quakers, as one of the most extreme left-wing sects within Puritanism, have unhappily become separated from it. In Richenda Scott's Swarthmore Lecture, she says, "With a simplicity almost sublime in its sweep... [George Fox] severed Quakerism from the main stream of Christian tradition and exploration and it has never yet found its way back."[11] And in 1954 Harold Loukes said that there will come a time when "the diverging stream of Quakerism must flow back into the main current."[12]

Chapter I

Each of the four types of modern Quakerism is leading the Society of Friends away from a sense of universal mission. Each has been willing to complacently accept the role of a small sect in a big world.

Catholic Quakerism*

The early Friends claimed that the truth that had been given them to proclaim was universal and that their faith was a catholic faith which was for all men to share. It is my aim to set forth the case for catholic Quakerism and to examine the foundations on which it was based.

The spirit of catholic Quakerism is given its classic expression in the opening sentence of the history of Quakerism written by Edward Burrough when the movement was only six years old. It is addressed "To all the world to whom this may come" and its stated purpose is that "they may come to the perfect knowledge of the ground of difference between ... all sects in these nations, and us who are in scorn called Quakers; showing that the controversy on our part is just and equal against them all, and that we have sufficient cause ... to deny their ministry, their church, their worship, and their whole religion, as being not in the power, and by the spirit of the living God, as commanded of him..." He declares that his aim is to show that "all the sects in these nations" have another "ground and foundation ... than that on which the true church, and ministry and practice, and worship and true religion were built in the days of the apostles."[13]

Burrough was not the only early Quaker to assert that Quakerism has another ground and foundation than all the several varieties of Protestantism. Penington declares that the Quakers "are not persons who have shot up out of the old root into another appearance, as one sect hath done out of another, till many are come up one after another, the ground still remaining the same out of which they all grew; but the ground hath been shaken ... in us; and the old root of Jesse hath been made manifest in us..."[14] Barclay says that though Protestants "have reformed from [the church of Rome] in some of the most gross points, and absurd doctrines, ... yet (which is to be regretted)

---

* See note on page 1. "Catholic" here means "universal and inclusive."

they have but lopt the branches, but retain and plead earnestly for the same root..."[15] And George Fox says, "The Quakers are of the seed of Abraham, of that seed in which all the nations are blessed, and of the faith of Abraham and never came from the several Protestants nor Papists neither from their evil root nor stock..."[16]

Fox and the early Quakers believed that their faith grew from an entirely different root system from that which nourished the several Protestant denominations, and because of this they saw Quakerism not as a branch of Protestantism but as a new thing, which, because it springs from another root, must be seen as a whole new conception of Christianity.

As Fox read the Bible he was impressed by the way God takes the initiative in his dealings with men in history. Abraham did not plan to take a stand at the headwaters of a stream that would eventually cover the whole earth with God's blessing. David became the ruler over God's people through a series of events that he could not have planned himself, yet he became the symbol of God's kingly rule and implanted in the Hebrew people a perennial hope for another king like him.

The coming of Jesus is an event in which God again takes the initiative and brings something new into the world. But Jesus' coming is not just one of a series of God-initiated events. The Jesus event is a *covenant* event. It brings in a whole *new* way to God.

The old way and covenant was established through God-initiated events, and the Hebrew people looked back on these events as the beginnings of the law and the God-ruled society. But the new way and new covenant community, though it also has a beginning through God's revelation in history, is not simply the lengthened shadow of that first initiatory event, but it is an event that can be experienced again and again. It is an event that does not fade with the passage of time. It is not something that was new once and then began to become old. It has the quality of perpetual newness. The priest of this new covenant is like the mysterious Melchizedek whose priesthood is never ending and whose consecration is perpetual. He is able to save to the uttermost all who come to God by him for he is a living intercessor—the same yesterday, today, and forever.

Chapter I

The new covenant way to God is not a way of new cultus or a new law but it is a master-disciple relationship to Jesus Christ, who is not the dead founder of the Christian religion, but one who confronts us today with his call "Follow me" and who creates by his presence in all his offices a new covenant community. Christian morality and Christian community exist only by virtue of a person-to-person relationship to the living Christ and they do not exist apart from this relationship.

Over against this vision of a religion-less way to God stands the "Christian religion" which, according to Fox, is a creation of man and has its roots in human inventiveness and not in the free act of God. Fox claimed that this Christian religion began to make its appearance "in the apostles' days." By the time Christianity had become a state religion with the Bishop of Rome as its autocratic head, this man-made Christianity had become a system of religion which completely eclipsed the new way to God that Christ had inaugurated. For early Quakers this transformation from faith to religion was symbolized by the pope and the whole system of man-made Christianity was called "popery."

For early Quakers the significance of the Reformation of the 16th century was to be found in its movement away from the "pope's inventions"[17] and toward the restoration of "the pure religion, that comes down from above, which is not of man's making; but comes down from God."[18] Penington says, "...the Lord God ... could not but expect that the reformation should grow and increase until ... nothing were left which arose from that spirit from which Popery sprang..."[19] And he sadly observes that "the reformation out of Popery was not pursued as the Lord expected it should!" and "there was a going backwards toward Popery again, instead of going further from it."[20]

"The spirit of Popery" is regarded as the enemy of true faith, and this spirit is that which seeks to create a system of religion in place of the religion-less new covenant. "The spirit of Popery" is therefore something which is not to be identified solely with the Roman Catholic tradition. The object of the Quaker mission was to proclaim the religion-less new covenant over against both the Roman Catholic and Protestant systems of Christianity. Fox says that since the apostles' days "false churches appeared as papists and protestants, no difference in nature..."[21] And Edward Burrough says, "the Protestant church, and worship, and ministry, are not another in nature and being, than the Romish Church, ministry and worship, but are sprung therefrom as branches out of the same root, the ground being one and the same though differing in appearance."[22] Penington states further that it is not only conservative Protestantism that springs from the same ground and root as the Romish church, but radical Protestantism springs from this root also. In his view, "the Papists and all pretended Christians (of the same spirit) who feel not the true Spirit, power and life, are but one in the ground, how great soever their differences outwardly, seem. And those that separate further and further (even to the utmost extent outwardly, or in a way of appearance) being not separated by the Lord from that nature and spirit wherein the enmity lodgeth, they are still inhabitants of one and the same city (for the city of Babylon is very large)."[23] Fox says to his Protestant critics "the Quakers are neither of you ... nor of the pope"[24] but "are risen up in the night of apostasy, and discover you all, what you are in, and what you went from..."[25]

Fox believed that it was his God-given task to "bring people off ... from men's inventions."[26] He says, "Now, when the Lord God and his son, Jesus Christ, did send me forth into the world, to preach his everlasting gospel and kingdom, I was glad that I was commanded ... to bring people off from all their own ways to Christ, the new and living way, and from their churches, which men had made and gathered, to the Church in God ... which Christ is the head of, and off from the world's teachers made by men, to learn of Christ, who is the way, the truth and the life, of whom the Father said 'This is my beloved Son, hear ye him...'" [27]

Many more citations could be produced to show that the Quakers saw their message and mission as something distinct from Protestantism in all its many forms. This does not mean that Quakerism and Puritanism have nothing in common for there are a number of striking instances of common characteristics. But the Quakers have a different principle or strategy of reformation. They have a different "ground and root" even from those Puritan separatists who had reformed themselves "to the utmost extent outwardly." If we fail to understand the "ground and root" of the early Quaker interpretation of Christianity we will get a distorted view of the trunk and the branches.

In order to understand Catholic Quakerism in all its comprehensiveness one must be willing to make the effort to look at Christianity with new eyes and to see it as a new thing. For those who are steeped in the Roman Catholic or Protestant traditions this requires nothing less than a major reorientation to the Christian revelation.

The Ground, Root and Foundation

The first step toward making this new approach is to grasp the meaning of the ground, root and foundation of the Quakers' faith and distinguish it from the ground, root and foundation of the Roman Catholic and Protestant traditions.

This new approach begins with belief in God who created all things out of nothing and who created man as a being with whom he could converse. Man is a being whose creator visits him and speaks to him, demanding a reply. Brunner says, "God has a different relation to man from what he has to other creatures ... He has intercourse with man; He reveals His will to him and expects obedience and trust from him. It is not that man as he is in himself bears God's likeness, but, rather, that man is designated for, and called to, a particular relation with God."[28] Fox says that men and women were happy as long as they "stood in the counsel of God and in obedience to his heavenly voice and command ... I say, as long as men and women stood in God's counsel and in obedience to his word ... they stood in God's righteous holy image."[29] "Man feels not the happiness but as he is in the power of God, in which he has communion with him."[30]

The life which is in dialogue with the creator is a life that is full of light because "God is light and in him is no darkness at all." The life that is lived apart from God's counsel and obedience to his word is a life of darkness. Light and darkness are not two opposing principles that struggle to dominate the universe from opposite poles. But man's life is torn between light and darkness.

The conversational relationship with God for which man was designated is essential to man's life. When this relationship is broken the ground of man's life is broken and instead of life he knows only death. When man is separated from the word that God speaks to him then death and darkness overtake him.

It is not some special kind of life that comes to man through conversation with his creator—such as "the religious life" "spiritual life" or "the mystical life". This conversational relationship is the condition of *life itself*. Brunner says that "in the Biblical revelation the concern is not only—as in other religions—with communication of some knowledge which is important for life, but with life itself. The darkness of which the revelation makes an end is death, disaster, ruin, destruction; the light which it brings is salvation and life. Revelation is the communication of life, not merely the intensification of life that already exists…"[31]

There is no coming out of darkness and death while man is alienated from God and does not listen to his word or fails to obey his command. This dialogic relationship to God is not a special religious consciousness but it is the basic law of man's being.

Three Essentials

There are three things that are essential to the life of man which are lacking when he fails to listen to God and obey his word.

The *first* is moral rectitude or what the Bible calls righteousness. This includes a knowledge of what is right and what is wrong, and the power to choose the right and reject the wrong.

The *second* essential is the necessity to live in a God-created community. God did not create man to live alone and man cannot create a man-made community from human resources alone. Unity and community come from above. They are the gift of God. All attempts to build a human society apart from God's wisdom and help are destined to fail because, says Suzanne De Dietrich, "all tensions and disruptions of mankind go back to a fundamental disruption produced by the *will to autonomy* of the creature as over against the Creator."[32] The God whom we know in history as the God who speaks has all along been calling for a righteous holy people to live under his rule. When he speaks to me and when I answer in obedience then I am no longer alone, for I am bound to all the others who have heard his call and answered it.

The *third* essential thing is to find our right relationship to the created world. The Bible does not view man's natural environment as neutral and plastic and always subject to human control. The non-human world around us can be friendly and serve us or it can be our enemy and enslave us. The book of Genesis tells us that God intends man to have dominion over his natural surroundings. This domination over the created world can be enjoyed when man orders the life around him by the wisdom of God that is revealed within him. To seek to order the creation outside of God's wisdom can only lead to the loss of man's happiness or even his very existence. One of the frequently recurring themes in science fiction, from *Frankenstein* onwards, is the possibility that a too clever manipulation of natural resources may lead to dire results for the manipulators. For 100 years the spirit of rationalistic science, technique, and economy has dominated the life of western man. We have witnessed the attempt of finite man to order his existence entirely within the limits of his finitude. Men are already beginning to experience fear as they contemplate the consequences of all this. In the next hundred years the people of God may find that this is the chief area in which they are called to witness.

A Dialogic Relationship To God

Fox sees the redemptive purpose of God in sending Christ into the world to consist in bringing men back to the original dialogic relationship to himself. He sees that the whole story of God's dealings with men in history from Abraham onward signifies that God wants men who find fellowship in hearing and obeying.

The law which came by Moses stands for God's holy word, and the descendants of Abraham, as the people of the law, are the people who live by this word from God. And yet there is a difference between obedience to this law and the life of communion with God that the prophets experienced. There is something static about obedience to the law, given once for all, whereas in the prophet's life, which is open toward God, there is a dynamic relationship to God who reveals his will in relation to the problems raised by a changing historical situation. The scrupulous observer of the legal code may be living a life that is far removed from the obedience that God is calling for in his particular life situation.

Therefore, for Fox, obedience is not to be understood in relation to a static legal code but must rather be understood in terms of a dynamic conversational relationship with the God who speaks. God's law is not a thing, an "it", but it is a relationship involving a divine speaker who must be heard and answered. Fox frequently uses the term "the life of the law" and by this he means the life of hearing and obeying. Fox observes that the prophets are not merely faithful observers of the Mosaic law but that they experienced and advocated a closer approach to God. This closer approach is what Fox means by the "life of the law." This is more than a mere legal rectitude. He also calls this more dynamic experience "the spirit and power that the prophets and apostles were in".

That which the prophets and apostles had in common was the spirit of hearing and obeying the voice of the creator. Fox says, "all the prophets and ... apostles were attentive and obedient to this heavenly voice."[33] The term "life" as Fox uses it is the relationship in which man is hearer and God is speaker. Fox says, "he that is kept in the life, hears God,"[34] and of those who do not hearken to the life he says, "they being from the life could not hear ... the life, when the life spake to them."[35]

Fox maintains that the coming of Christ is for the purpose of making this life of hearing and obeying a universal possibility by which a new righteousness and new community will be established on Christ the one foundation. God's new covenant people are founded on the prophets and apostles, Jesus Christ being the chief cornerstone. The great apostasy to which Fox frequently referred was from "the life the apostles were in, and the prophets."[36]

Christ is the light of the world by which the original dialogic relationship to God is being restored, and Fox says, "Hearken to the light ... whereby you may come to the life of the prophets..."[37]

Chapter I

The Quaker movement had as its ground, root and foundation a fervent desire to experience, through Christ, the God who speaks, and to become one with the prophets and apostles in the experience of hearing and obeying. Apart from this life there is no pleasing God. To the Christian world of his day Fox puts this challenge, "You have had the name of christians, which name hath come by tradition and succession ... but the life, and the power, and the love, and the wisdom that was among the apostles ... have you ... been out of generally, and it is in the life and power of God in which God is served."[38]

Fox says that Christ's covenant of light is not a new law, a new cultus, a new system of religion, but a restoration of the original dialogic relationship that God intended for man when he created him. The word of the Lord came to Isaiah saying, "I will lead them into paths that they have not known."[39] For Fox the newness of the new covenant consists in its new foundation, Jesus Christ, who is the prophet who speaks from heaven and who is the way in which God's spirit that had formerly fallen chiefly on the prophets will be poured out upon all flesh. That which distinguished the new covenant from the old is that the old has as its base and foundation a "something," an "it" which is the law and the cultus; whereas the new covenant is rooted and grounded in a master-disciple relationship to the living Christ. Fox says, "It is the life that differs, and the new way differs from the old, and the religion that is above, from that which is below."[40] In 1647 the Lord "opened" to him, "That which people do trample upon must be thy food. And as the Lord spoke he opened it to me how that people and professors did trample upon the life, even the life of Christ was trampled upon; and they fed upon words, and fed one another with words, but trampled upon the life..."[41] "Serve God in newness of life," he exhorts, "for it is the life, and a living and walking in the truth, that must answer the witness of God In all people."[42]

The True And Sure Foundation

Traditional and nominal Christianity has trampled upon this life but, says Fox, "the Quakers are ... in the life of all the prophets, apostles and Christ"[43] and he asserts that the Quakers "are come to witness the life that Moses was in, and the prophets were in, and David was in."[44] In Christ, God has given us the perfect way to restore the lost dialogic relationship. Fox says, "Many foundations have been laid since the apostles' days, by such as are gone from Christ the true and sure Foundation."[45] Such he calls "gadders abroad from God, out of the life."[46]

He maintains that Christ "was the foundation of the holy prophets and apostles... and is the foundation of all his holy people now."[47] He calls Christ a "living rock and foundation"[48] and he declares that "Christ, who is your foundation... is razing down to the ground the world's foundation; ... and is setting up himself, the living and everlasting foundation, for all his to build upon ... He will shake the foundations of all false religions, ways, worships, churches, and teachers and will make the pillars of them to totter."[49] "God laid the foundation ... Christ Jesus. When wise men are turned backward ... and all makers of trades of Christ and the apostles' words... fall, the foundation of God, Christ Jesus, remains; they who are built on him are sure and remain."[50]

So there is a foundation, root and ground of the Quakers' message, and it is on the basis of this foundation, root and ground that the Quakers asked to be understood.

Penington sums it up in these words, "...there was a falling away... and a very great and universal apostasy from the Spirit and power of the apostles ... many ... holding a form of Godliness out of the power. But God ... determined to send an angel to preach his everlasting gospel again; and in due time so did... (None could preach the gospel after the apostasy by any ordination or succession of ministry left amongst men but there must be a new receiving of the gospel, by a new message and commission from on high) ... he that hath a heart opened by the Lord, let him acknowledge it."[51]

Chapter II

The Quaker Understanding of Christian Ethics

Prophetic faith bears witness to one God who made all things and who calls men to righteousness. What is the nature of this righteousness?

What the Bible calls righteousness and what we are discussing here as Christian ethics can have several different meanings. For some it means that the Christian religion has a "morals department" which consists of certain moral principles and rules of conduct, which are binding on all Christians in the way that the Mosaic Law is binding on the Jews. For others, there is a universal moral law that is built into the structure of the universe, and Christianity is one pathway that leads to it. Where the moral law is believed to exist apart from any particular revelation from God, this leads to the presumption that morality can be made the subject of scientific analysis, and that it is possible to produce a "science of morals" by this means.

It is presumed here that Christian morality is based on God's revelation in Jesus Christ. But even when morality is believed to have its source in divine revelation there are different ways of looking at it. I want to focus attention on the contrast between the *ethic of obligation* and the *ethic of idealism*.

The *ethic of idealism* starts with ideal social ends or goals, and it sees religion as a force leading to the realization of these goals. The Christian idealist sees morality as the struggle to attain ultimate moral goals, and he finds a wide gulf between these ultimate goals and immediate practical possibilities and available moral energies. For the Christian idealist a standard of Christian morals can have validity quite apart from our present capacity to bring our lives into conformity with it. There is therefore, in Christian moral idealism, a gap between the ultimate moral good and the Christian's present ability to live up to it. This approach takes it for granted that there can be an unresolvable tension between what a Christian knows he ought to do and what, in fact, he is able to do.

The *ethic of obligation*, on the other hand, sees right action as a response to God's command. It begins with the assertion, "He hath showed thee, O man, what is good..." This approach raises a number of questions: How is God's will revealed to us? Is it through the Bible? the conscience? the church? the holy spirit? Does it come to each individual as a private revelation of the right way for him alone, thus dividing and scattering Christians on the level of moral action, or does it make the same moral demands on all, so that the act of obedience strengthens the fellowship and draws it into closer unity? If God speaks with one voice to all, does this lead to legalism and rigid discipline, or can freedom be experienced along with corporate obedience? As God's people answer his moral demands, should this lead them to a style of life that stands out in bold contrast to the general culture of the people "who know not God"? Or should they try to create a cultural synthesis in which religious morality and secular values are blended into one whole? Should the church which is committed to live in obedience to God's word conceive its role as the furnisher of moral standards to secular society and the custodian of public morals? Or should it see itself as salt and leaven to society in general, not only by making official pronouncements on moral issues, but by witnessing to the divine imperative through corporate obedience and suffering?

Righteousness and Community

The early Quaker view of Christian ethics rests upon two basic beliefs: first, that God's call to righteousness is experienced through a master–disciple relationship to Christ, and, second, that God's call to community is experienced through coming under the authority and headship of Christ. Righteousness and community furnish the central core around which Fox's whole conception of Christianity revolves. Fox's Christian ethic is an ethic of obligation and not an ethic of idealism. The call to righteousness is a call to do something or to refrain from doing something, and that which the eternal voice commands is never beyond our power to obey. Fox says, "God is equal and righteous, and commands nothing but what is equal and just, and measurable, according to that which men may perform;... God is not unrighteous, or a hard taskmaster, to lay more upon a man than he can do...as to command them to do the thing they cannot..."[1] "...neither Christ nor God commended anything but what should be attained unto and it will be attained unto and hath been attained unto."[2] "Christ will lay no more upon you than you are able to bear."[3]

The gap between the vision of moral truth and the power to do it is the bugbear of Protestant ethics, but it is totally absent from the teaching of Fox, Penn and Penington. This leaves no room for the plea, "I know what God wants me to do but I haven't the power to do it." The choice is between obedience and disobedience. There is no third position where man is suspended between a vision of moral truth and a lack of moral power to perform it. Penington says, "as the soul in faith gives itself up to obey, so the power appears and works the obedience...the power never fails the faith."[4] And Penn says, "...if men are wicked, not because they will not do better; but because they neither see nor know, nor are able to do better; how heavy, how black, how blasphemous a character doth the consequence of these men's opinions fasten upon the righteous God of Heaven and Earth since it supposes him not to have given either inwardly or outwardly unto men means sufficient to do what he requires of them..."[5]

In Fox's day, the Puritan version of Calvinism maintained that Jesus' power to save is a power that does not break the power of sin over us in this earthly life. Fox maintained that Jesus came not to save us in our sins but from our sins. He also questioned the Roman Catholic doctrine that Christ's power is not sufficient to purge us of sin and that, therefore, we must pass through a special purgative experience after death.

In modern times there are still plenty of Protestant spokesmen who are ready to "plead for sin." One such is John Knox, who says that for the Christian the ethical problem is a "perplexing" one. "This problem is created by his recognition, on the one hand, of the absolute truth of Jesus' ethical teachings and, on the other, of his own inability to keep them. No serious person who has ever begun to see the meaning or feel the force of Jesus' teachings and life can escape this predicament. This impracticability of an ethical ideal in whose ultimate truth we cannot avoid feeling the fullest confidence, constitutes the essential problem of Christian ethics."[6] "...we are the slaves of sin—that is, we are prevented by forces beyond our power to control from fulfilling the righteousness that we know to be the law of our own being—and we are incapable of extricating ourselves from our plight."[7]

The early Quakers took their stand in opposition to this position. This is the much discussed "Quaker doctrine of perfection." "Perfection," as early Quakers used this term, means only that when God commands we can both hear and obey; and when we hear and obey we are fulfilling the law of our being as perfectly as is humanly possible.

This belief that Christ teaches us the principles of God's righteousness and gives us the power to obey them is the greatest single factor in the formation of "the Quaker character."

It has already been pointed out that there is a variety of ways of answering the question, "How does God speak to us?" Here, again, we need to remember that Fox believed that throughout the whole history of prophetic religion God has been calling for righteousness and community. Therefore, when Fox read the words "I am the way," it could only mean to him that Christ is the new and living way to God's righteousness and God's community. When Jesus said, "I am the light of the world," it could only mean to Fox that righteousness and community are to be given us through Christ. But how does this righteousness of God reach us through Christ? Fox rejects most of the usual answers. The Bible he rejects because to make Jesus' moral teachings into a new Torah would be no new way. Conscience he rejects because it is the receiver and not the giver of moral truth. The church as an external institutional controller of morals will not do because this is one of the oldest of human methods to control public morality. The holy spirit would surely be accepted by Fox as a moral authority, but not in any sense that would make it distinct from Christ and independent of his authority.

Christ, the Teacher of Righteousness

If the saints are to be brought to perfection, which means to live in obedience to the righteousness of God, then they will be taught this righteousness by Christ himself. This is Fox's mighty proclamation, that "Christ has come to teach his people himself."[8] Christ is the teacher of righteousness and holiness. It is because he does this that he is the light. Fox asks, "Doth not the Light that lighteth every man that cometh into the world, bring in the righteousness of God?"[9] "The light doth exercise the conscience towards God and towards man, which light cometh from Christ."[10] This light, he says, "corrects you that are in the legal righteousness, and out of Christ."[11]

Fox sees the appearance of Christ as the teacher of righteousness to God's people as the means by which God is restoring the original relationship of dependence for which man was created. Man was created to live by hearing and obeying God's word which is light. But this original light is not a part of the created universe; it is only experienced in the form of a dialogue between man and his creator. Fox says, "the light Adam had before the fall did not come by the creation, nor by the things that are made."[12] The original light that was before the darkness is to be understood as the voice of the creator. But the light that came to shine again in the darkness is also an uncreated light. Christ's voice, which is the saving light from the creator, comes to us with the authority of the creator. Fox says, "The light, which every man that cometh into the world is enlightened with ... is Christ, by whom the world was made, ... the creation was made by him, and he was before it was made, so he is not a created light, but that by which all things were created."[13] And so Fox is able to say of the light of Christ, "they that hear the light, hear that which was from the beginning."[14]

The light is a voice which must be heard and obeyed. "This light," says Fox, "it speaks to you."[15] Fox speaks of *hearing* the light at least thirty-five times, and this is not so illogical when we remember that, for Fox, darkness is alienation from the voice of

The Quaker Understanding of Christian Ethics

the creator.

The light, then, does not lead us to an abstract moral philosophy, but we experience it as the sound of a voice that speaks to us in the tone of a command. This light, says Fox, "if you love it will lead you to know Christ's voice and when it doth command."[16] "After you have heard the light, believe and obey."[17] "Ye that turn from the light, turn from the command of God."[18]

Christ, the light, is related to God's people in the new covenant in the way that the prophets were related to God's people in the old covenant. Fox agrees with Peter, Stephen, and the author of Hebrews that Christ fulfilled Moses' prophecy: "A prophet like me will the Lord raise up—him you will hear in all things—they that do not obey him will be condemned." Fox says, "everyone ... which hears not the light, the light which doth enlighten him, he hears not the prophet which Moses prophesied of; so the light condemns him..."[19]

The Consequences of a Personal Relationship with Christ

From the foregoing sketch of Fox's view of Christian ethics it should be evident that he understands the Christian's moral life as proceeding from a dynamic personal relationship with Jesus Christ, whose word is experienced as a divine command that can and must be obeyed.

There are several consequences that flow from this doctrine upon which Fox lays special emphasis.

First, the assurance that the ultimate principles of God's righteousness are revealed and *power to obey is available.*

This releases the maximum of moral energy. Unlike the scrupulosity of the moralist and the over-straining for consistency of the idealist, this kind of moral exercise does not produce warped personalities, nor reduce the reserves of energy, thus weakening the capacity for further moral effort. Hearing and obeying the voice of the creator is the fundamental law of man's being, and it is by this exercise that he comes closest to fulfilling the purpose for which he was created (i.e., to glorify God and keep his commandments). This kind of moral energy is not consumed with the using but rather builds up from strength to strength.

Second, this encounter with moral truth is not a private experience. God does not speak with two voices. The word of moral truth that comes to one comes to all. Fox says, "this way of holiness that the prophets prophesied of is Christ Jesus, the way,"[20] and he observes that the call of God is that "all may walk in holiness as becomes the house of God."[21] The turning of God's people to one living authority who teaches the same moral truth to all is an experience that brings all into unity. Fox says, "in the holiness is the unity,"[22] and that the saints are to "walk in unity over the enmity."[23]

The proclamation that "Christ has come to teach his people" means that obedience in righteousness is an experience that binds the individual Christian to all the other children of obedience. Fox says that where the light is loved "here no self can stand, but it is judged with the light; and here all are in unity."[24]

The *third* characteristic of the Quaker understanding of Christian ethics is that which Fox called the "pure", "spiritual", "divine", "righteous", "holy" liberty of the gospel. Fox's teaching about Christian liberty is of special interest because it is at this point that Quaker ethics deviate sharply from the position of other Christian groups who have accepted the call of Christ for corporate obedience in righteousness by the whole church. Where this call of Christ is accepted it becomes necessary to find a common standard of righteousness to which the whole Christian community has access, and a disciplinary procedure by which the whole church can come to unity. The Bible has usually furnished the standard of corporate righteousness for such groups. Several disciplinary procedures have appeared. Sometimes certain church officers are invested with disciplinary authority. The disciplinary officer has certain powers—he can insist on public confession of error, he can invoke social ostracism (avoidance or shunning), or resort to excommunication if the confession is not forthcoming. In other systems the disciplinary officer plays a small part and discipline rests on a primary confessional commitment to subordinate the will of the individual to the will of the group. Here again social ostracism and excommunication are instruments of discipline, but they are used at the discretion of the whole group instead of delegated officers. Where the righteousness of God is learned by studying a book, and where the unity in righteousness is achieved by social machinery involving human authority, we can expect that this situation will tend to foster spiritual pride and create a power structure in which the power of God is reduced to the terms of human authority.

In this kind of situation the Christian in search of the righteousness of God, and fellowship with others in obedience to that righteousness, is confronted with the authority of the Bible and the authority of the religious institution. Righteousness becomes understood as something external to the individual Christian and God's dealings with the individual Christian. Righteousness becomes based on authoritative sacred writings and an authoritative holy community. This approach avoids subjectivity and individualism by putting the whole basis of righteousness outside the inner experience of the individual Christian. By identifying righteousness with book and community it thereby makes it an object separate from the individual Christian to which he must yield and submit. This approach can produce a certain moral solidarity in a Christian group.

However, it has dangerous side effects. In this kind of religious environment the Christian feels boxed in. A tension is set up between the individual and the group, and the cards are stacked in such a way that the individual cannot win. His attitude toward the group may become defeatist, or he may keep alive an inner resistance that does not show on the surface but leaves his inner life divided and at war with itself. Where punitive discipline is repeatedly applied the spirit becomes wounded, or it may be forced into an unnatural docility. People are drawn into this kind of community through a desire to follow Christ and to become gathered into a fellowship that is obedient to him in all things. But as time goes on they become haunted by the suspicion that conformity to the authority of book and community is filling their whole lives and preventing, rather than fostering, the experience of following the master. Jesus spoke of freedom and liberty, but in this kind of church community freedom and liberty seem to be rarely experienced, and the individual does not have the exhilarating sense of having been brought into the glorious liberty of the sons of God.

One way to escape from the excesses of a too rigid church discipline is to let the pendulum swing to the opposite extreme and to assert the supremacy of the individual over the group, and to create a fellowship so loose that in all matters of tension between the individual and the group the cards will be stacked so that the group cannot win. In this way the wounds, repressions and frustrations resulting from rigid discipline are successfully avoided, but the resultant individualism prevents the community from having a clear sense of purpose or even a sense of direction. In the end it can only offer a satisfying fellowship to those for whom individualism in religion is a primary good. The vision of a righteous, holy community living in unity under God's rule must be abandoned.

Both Quakers and others often make the mistake of supposing that Fox stood for the kind of liberty that leaves the individual an absolutely independent agent and makes the church fellowship a loose association of such free agents. Fox's position is neither that of a rigid discipline based on the authority of book or community, nor of a loose individualism that is unconcerned about the problem of Christian unity.

Christian Liberty

What Fox has to say about Christian liberty is one of the most important aspects of his teaching.

At the beginning of this study we observed that, in Fox's view, man is a being who was created to live in a relationship of dependence to his creator. Because of this basic fact of man's existence he has no possibility of experiencing absolute freedom. Fox is not the first or the last to hold this view. Brunner says, "The being of God alone is unconditioned, absolute freedom; that of the creature is conditioned, relative freedom, freedom in dependence ... Because the being of man is actually based upon man's dependence upon God, upon the Call of God which chooses him and gives him responsibility, his freedom is only complete where he remains in this dependence, hence ... the maximum of his dependence on God is at the same time the maximum of his freedom..."[25]

Penington says, "as for your speaking of free will, ye do not know what you speak of: for the will with the freedom of it either stands in the image and power of him that made it or in a contrary image and power ... The will is not of itself but stands in another, and is the servant to that in whom it stands and there its freedom is found and comprehended. For there is no middle state between both, wherein the will stands of itself and is free to both equally, but it is a servant and under the command of one of these powers ... such free will as men commonly speak of is mere imagination..."[26]

Fox says, "do not think that I hold free will here, man's free will, I speak of that which is contrary to man's will, and loving the light it will keep your wills ... in subjection."[27]

"Free will ... [is] out of the light which is Christ..."[28] "Stand in the will of God, with thy own will offered up as his was who said, 'Not my will but thine'..."[29]

The beginning of the understanding of liberty is that the only real liberty open to us is a kind of subjection. Fox says that true liberty is only found through Christ, the way, but that we must use this liberty as the servants of God.

We can hear and obey the voice of the creator who speaks in the accents of steadfast love, or we can hear and obey the tempter whose purpose is to destroy us. Fox says, "Whose servant thou art, whom thou dost obey, whether it be sin unto death, or of obedience unto righteousness."[30]

On the surface this looks like a false choice—either way it leads to servitude and subjection. But in actual experience these two kinds of obedience lead to exactly opposite consequences. The one leads to liberty and freedom; the other leads to captivity and bondage.

Gospel Freedom

In Fox's teaching great emphasis is laid on the freedom that belongs to the gospel and new covenant. Fox says, "in this gospel (the power of God ...) is the true liberty,"[31] and they whose faith stands in the gospel "are made God's free men and women."[32] "By this grace and truth in the new covenant, all may be made

Chapter II

God's free men and women, to serve God in the new life, and in the new and living way; ..."[33] That which "is ... not in the Spirit of God nor in his gospel... its liberty is in the darkness: for all the true liberty is in the gospel and the truth that makes free; ..."[34]

This gospel freedom is, for Fox, a major part of our heritage in the gospel. "Whom the Lord hath called..." he says, "are the Lord's freemen,"[35] "...they are free citizens, they are freeholders of an everlasting inheritance, so they are not captives, they are not bondmen, they are not servants nor slaves. But (mark) free men and women. And what hath made them free men, and free women, but truth?"[36] "And the truth is Christ and Christ is the truth."[37] "...it is Christ the truth that doth set free."[38] For Fox true Christian character does not consist in docile conformity to righteousness based on the letter of scripture and enforced by institutional church discipline. Group solidarity in obedience to righteousness does not weaken individuality if the emphasis is laid where Fox laid it. Fox says, "the gospel brings a man to be a man,"[39] and "truth makes a man a man."[40]

The bad psychological consequences of a legalistic conception of righteousness and a too rigid church discipline can be avoided if we take seriously the proclamation, "Christ has come to teach his people himself." This means that Christ is teaching both individuals *and* "his people" the righteousness which God has all along been calling for. He teaches with authority and what he teaches one, he teaches all. His word to us is not a mere subjective intimation, because it comes to us as the word of him by whom all things were made and created. He speaks with authority and we are bound to obey him. In this act of obedience the people of God in the new covenant find the basis or ground of their fellowship. Fox says, "all christians that own God and Christ Jesus, and his gospel, which is the power of God, ... ought to have the liberty of the gospel, for the liberty ... is in Christ."[41] Liberty is not opposed to unity, but in the gospel and new covenant they appear together. Fox says, "in the liberty of the Spirit there is the unity ... and all are one in Christ Jesus, in whom is the true liberty."[42]

Corporate Obedience

The call to be a righteous holy people under God's rule is to be answered, not by an extraordinary burst of human effort, but by the "power of God," that is, by the gospel which is the power of God. Liberty is not the right to contract out of corporate obedience in righteousness, but Christian liberty and corporate obedience in righteousness belong together. This liberty is never an excuse to relax our resolution to find the unity in obedience that God calls for. Fox exhorts all to stand fast in the righteous holy liberty of Christ that has freed them from all loose and false liberty.[43]

The Quaker approach to corporate obedience is not reinforced by such churchly weapons as shunning, avoidance, excommunication, etc. Brothers in Christ are to watch over one another for good and, if unity is to be maintained, much time will be spent in dealing with those children of the light who lag behind in walking in the light. But the Quaker method of Christian admonition is to stir up the laggard to "turn again to that of which you were first convinced," which means to the conviction that Christ really does teach his people and lead them into all truth. The authority is Christ's and the compulsion to obey ought always to come from him. Something all wrong happens when the church assumes the role of commander and enforcer; then the disciple feels the pressure of some yoke other than the easy yoke of Christ. The aim of church discipline is not to force the individual to conform to the group, but to stir up the individual to more faithful obedience to him who is leading all God's people to walk in unity and sameness of mind.

Fox rejects excommunication as non-apostolic[44] and "not found in the scriptures of truth."[45] The Quaker practice of disownment does not prohibit social relationships nor bar the disowned person from public meetings for worship. It is an act of formal announcement addressed to "the world," stating that the person named is not in fellowship with the Quaker community. The purpose of disownment is not punitive, but so that "the miscarriages of some may not be charged on the body of Friends,"[46] and so "that no reproach may come or rest on God's holy name, truth and people."[47]

Chapter II

Fox advises that decisions to disown should be unanimous, and later practice made it possible for the disowned to appeal to the quarterly and yearly meetings. Fox's approach to church discipline is in the spirit of his statement: "The law woundeth: but the gospel healeth."[48] The process of finding the unity in righteousness that God calls for requires much patience and tenderness and must never be viewed as the enforcement of church law. In the Quaker experience it is not the will of the group, but the will of God that stands over against self will.

When the group takes measures to draw all into unity what is happening is not the weight of the many tipping the scale against the weight of the one. It is therefore misleading to speak of the Quaker concept of church discipline as the application of a "group check." If the church does not represent the mind of Christ it cannot check anything at all. In so far as the church can influence the individual to turn to Christ and learn of him, it is building up that unity that Christ is leading his people toward. But the individual also may be required sometimes to turn the group to Christ, as John Woolman did.

Where every disciple desires to live the life of discipleship in unity with all the other disciples there should be no unhealthy feeling of social pressure on the individual, and no sense of conflict between the individual Christian and the Christian community. However, where the individual has not learned, like Fox, to "give up self to die by the cross,"[49] he will feel even the gentlest church discipline as a threat to his individuality. S. R. Hopper says that, "Self-will looks upon obedience to God as something which would bind it; sees it not as a relationship of living communion whereby we are empowered to realize God's idea of us, but sees God as law which bends us to his ultimate control."[50]

Fox's understanding of Christian ethics leads to a view of the church in which the ground of fellowship is found in the experience of corporate obedience in ethics. Corporate obedience to the head of the church creates a community with a style of life, or pattern of life, that differs from the style of life of those communities who do not know Christ as head. The Christian Community as Fox envisaged it is a community that stands committed to certain definite leadings that it has received from

Christ which are binding on the whole fellowship. These leadings can sometimes be in direct conflict with certain forms of behavior demanded by the secular or religious institutions of society. When such conflicts develop into a crisis situation the church is called to suffer as a community, and Fox calls this suffering church "the church of Christ's cross."[51] Fox sees the coming of Christ as a manifestation of God's power—his power to teach us righteousness apart from legalism and give us community apart from institutionalism. Christ, by his example on the cross, shows us the way that God intends the church to release moral energies into the world: not by flaunting a superior moralism but by standing together and suffering for the sake of corporate obedience in righteousness.

The Role of the Church

And now, finally, we come to the last but not the least of the questions posed at the beginning: Should the church conceive of its role as the furnisher of moral standards for society in general?—or should it see itself called to be salt and leaven by witnessing to the divine imperative through corporate obedience and corporate suffering?

John Howard Yoder maintains that in the church of the cross "the Christian life is defined most basically in ethical terms. While forgiveness, membership in a social order, participation in worship, or receiving a revelation may all be very relevant factors they do not rob *obedience in ethics* (Nachfolge) of primary rank."[52]

The church that puts obedience in ethics before everything else soon finds itself in trouble. The world does not tolerate absolute ethical standards, and the church that attempts to live by such standards will be led into conflict with the standards and mores of society in general. The disciple church, says Yoder, is "an autonomous moral force representing in the midst of the world the demands of God's righteousness."[53]

Christian history offers few examples of the disciple church as Yoder describes it. From the fourth century to the present day, the majority of Christians have consciously adopted a position on Christian ethics that is very different from the position of the

Chapter II

disciple church. Yoder calls this other position "Constantinian." Constantinian Christianity accepts the tolerance, favor, protection, and support of the state. This means that the church ceases to be "a colony of heaven in a Christ-denying world," and, instead, it accepts the role of arbiter of morals for the social order of which it is a part. The Constantinian church is not a church of the cross. Its pact with political structures may take the form of a treaty between the church hierarchy and the state, or, as in America today, popular Christianity may become so imbedded in popular Americanism that when the church speaks it reflects, rather than challenges, the standards of worldly society. In either case the church ceases to be an autonomous moral force in the life of the nation.

The Constantinian point of view, says Yoder, is "built into the foundations of western social thinking."[54] It is a point of view which blurs the distinction between church and society and presupposes that Christian ethics "will have to apply as a simple, performable possibility for a whole society."[55]

From the standpoint of the Constantinian church the attitude of the disciple church towards Christian ethics is less than Christian. It calls the disciple church sectarian, and accuses it of having spiritual pride and employing a strategy of withdrawal. It is not merely that some who follow the way of the disciple church are guilty of spiritual pride. For a writer like Reinhold Niebuhr the whole disciple church vision and program is a manifestation of spiritual pride, and everyone connected with the disciple church is tainted with it.

The most frequent charge made against the disciple church is its "irresponsibility." The Constantinian church sees itself as supplying the moral backbone of society and accepting responsibility for the general moral tone of the nation in a way that the disciple church does not. The Constantinian church aims to be inclusive and to include within its borders the greatest possible proportion of the inhabitants of the nation. Its requirements for membership are not very demanding with respect to moral rectitude, and its pastoral oversight and church discipline touch the lives of its members very lightly or hardly at all. Consequently the experience of obeying together, witnessing together, and suffering together is not even a possibility in this type of church structure. Its moral influence is mediated chiefly, if not exclusively, through its institutional resources: through its literature, its priests, its preachers, its resolutions, its far-flung organizations and prestige.

Churches Of The Cross

The Reformation of the 16th century was not aimed at bringing the church out of the Constantinian tradition but was a movement for reform within that tradition. Within a decade of the beginnings of the Lutheran Reform there arose a powerful movement that advocated a complete break with the Constantinian tradition and accepted the role of a church of the cross. This Anabaptist movement appeared in strength in many parts of Europe and exhibited a missionary zeal such as the western church had not seen for over a thousand years. But this movement was vigorously repressed by Catholic and Protestant alike. Thousands were put to death and during this time of persecution most of the original leaders were killed.

The Anabaptist crusade to end the domination of the Constantinian conception of Christianity was successfully suppressed on the continent of Europe and has never been revived. The free church idea was reborn in Puritan England in the 17th century and later became the dominant religious force in North American Christianity. But a church, even though not legally allied to the secular power, can become domesticated into the secular culture, and this has largely been the fate of the "free" churches in America. The free church tradition, which now has such numerous progeny throughout the world, has never had a clear vision of the church of the cross, and it has left the witness to the possibility of corporate obedience and corporate suffering to Mennonites, Brethren and Quakers, whom it regards as radicals within its own tradition.

The large and historically important denominations in which the Constantinian spirit still prevails no longer persecute the churches of the cross. Disciple church theology is attacked by theologians like Reinhold Niebuhr, but the general attitude is one of toleration and even respect for a position which is seen as

Chapter II

going beyond what is required of the ordinary Christian. From this viewpoint it is possible to regard groups who practice corporate obedience and corporate suffering as belonging to a special witness to which God calls some Christians and not others. As the churches move closer and closer together by various types of mergers and ecumenical organizations, it has become natural for those churches who have not repudiated the Constantinian ideal to tolerantly regard the so-called "historic peace churches" as representing a special Christian vocation which could conceivably be recognized as having a place in their vision of reunited Christendom without tampering with existing Constantinian presuppositions. Some institutional churches have made a place for such groups and called them "orders." The proposal that the Quakers could naturally accept such a status in the emerging reunited church has appeared both within and without the Society. Such a proposal can only come as a result of a misunderstanding of the early Quaker vision and the implications of that vision for the future of Christianity.

The Quaker vision is for all men to share. The Quaker message is not a call to some and not to others. It cannot be relegated to the category of a form of "vocational Christianity" i.e., a form of Christianity which is good and true for some and not others.

George Fox expected that the vision of the church of the cross would replace both the Constantinian and "free church" conceptions of Christianity. The day when the Quakers accept the status of an order within a church structure based on Constantinian presuppositions will be the day when the early Quaker vision will cease to have any power to shape Christian history.

Chapter III

The Quaker Conception of Christian Community and Church Order

Of the two basic presuppositions in Fox's conception of Christianity we have already dealt with the first, namely, that God, through Christ, shows what is right and gives the power to do what is right. The second presupposition is that God is calling all men into a community whose fellowship and order are produced by a master-disciple relationship to the living Christ.

Man was created to live in a continuously dependent relationship to his Creator, and therefore hearing and obeying is the distinctively human activity. When man ceases to hear and obey, he falls from the position in which God has placed him. For Fox, Christianity means that God is restoring the original dialogic relationship.

The New Covenant Community

In the Mosaic covenant, law and cultus furnish the framework in which the Hebrew people were brought to a sense of being God's holy people who lived under his rule. But to know God through law and cultus is to know him at a point at least once removed from a "mouth to mouth" encounter with him. The Mosaic covenant was intended to prepare the way for another covenant that would restore the experience of hearing and obeying for all God's people. Fox interprets the coming of Christ as the appearance of this second covenant in which God is not approached through a legal code or cultic system, but solely through a conversational relationship to the living Christ. By this "new way" God is restoring the righteousness and community for which man was originally destined. This new covenant is God's

Chapter III

way of restoring to man the original dependent relationship which is constitutive of his manhood. The gospel is not that which makes a man to be religious, but it is that "which makes a man to be a man."[1] Fox believed that it was a part of his mission to proclaim the non-religious character of the new covenant. He claimed that the Christian revelation is most misunderstood when it is understood as bringing in a new religion.

Fox was not a religious reformer in the sense that he would have accepted the religious institutions of his day if they had been willing to adopt certain reforms. He maintained that the church of Jesus Christ is not a religious institution and that it is generically different from all religious institutions.

Fox is not the only opposer of ecclesiastical institutions. But most representatives of anti-ecclesiasticism have been individualists, or have held that the true church is invisible, or have advocated a church order based on rational or practical principles. Some build a community around a charismatic leader, while others resort to a dynastic conception of leadership. Fox is not an example of any of these types of anti-ecclesiasticism. He believed that there is an order that belongs to God's people in the new covenant. He calls this the Gospel order and he understands this new covenant community to have form, structure, order, and government without being a religious institution. It is an outwardly visible community with historical existence but not necessarily continuous historical existence. It owes its existence entirely to God's act in sending Christ into the world—in raising him from the dead and in making him head over the new covenant community. It does not despise order. It is not an anarchy. It is governed by a head whose authority is not distinct from the authority of the creator. It has social cohesion and functions as a social organism and not as a mere collective. It knows itself to be the people of a covenant no less than the people who received the law from the hands of Moses at Mount Sinai. It is conscious of a definite boundary between itself and the uncovenanted peoples. It believes itself to be the heir of the prophecies and promises. It has its roots in an historical event: the life, death and resurrection of Jesus Christ. It knows no new covenant or new covenant people apart from an experience of the risen Christ in a master–disciple relationship. The risen Christ brings to the new covenant people of God a knowledge of God's righteousness apart from the law, and he brings social cohesion apart from a cultic institution.

The voice of Christ that brings this new word must be obeyed because it is the voice of the creator. Christ is not compelled to speak to us. In coming to us he is not fulfilling some law of his being. But when he draws near to us we are under an absolute necessity to respond, for we have been created to live by his word and it is the law of our being so to do.

The Christ of day to day experience whom we know through faith is a living being. "He is therefore personal for it is as dynamic and sovereign will truly distinct from one's own will, that man comes to know him."* It is not that we experience the same spirit that was in the historical Jesus, so that the same spirit that filled him in unbounded measure now fills us in lesser measure. Nor do we meet Christ through a being, the Holy Ghost, who is not Christ but a representative of Christ who now deals with us instead of Christ. Nor is his encounter with us an encounter with abstract ideas which he taught and through which he continues to influence men.

No, Jesus' continued presence in the world is not one that follows some ordinary process by which great teachers continue to influence men and societies long after they are dead. Jesus' continued presence must be understood in terms of the new covenant between man and God that he established through the events of his death and resurrection. The head of the new covenant community of disciples is the resurrected Jesus, and it was the preaching of the resurrection that caused the first community of Christians to be gathered. The risen Christ is the prophet, priest, and king of the new covenant community. This community should not be understood as a cult centered on the belief in a beloved spiritual leader who rose from the dead.

The resurrection of Jesus is the resurrection of one who was the incarnation of the word that God speaks to man. He is the eternal prophet who speaks from heaven, and he speaks with the voice of authority because his voice is the voice of the creator. He

---

* The source of this quotation has not been found

is therefore "the light of men," and the new covenant established by his death and resurrection is the "covenant of light." God who is light and whose law is light has given men a covenant of light. In this new covenant the word and power of God are mediated to God's people through the risen Christ who is present in their midst. The new covenant is therefore not a legal code, cultus, or idea, but a person. The expected new covenant was to be a person: "I have given you as a covenant to the people, a light to the nations" was the prophetic word that came to Isaiah.*

This is the key to the new covenant community—it comes into existence when men hear and obey the voice of the living Christ, and it has no existence apart from this hearing and obeying. Faith is the ground of this community when faith is understood to mean putting one's whole existence under the authority of Christ. Fox said, "We are not our own, and are not to live to ourselves, nor to order ourselves, but to live unto him, and be ordered, ruled and governed by him."[2]

The life of this community is not sustained and upheld by perpetual ordinances and rules of succession. It is not a community that is started just once, in one place, and then expands from this one point. It is a community that comes into existence where faith exists and that withers and fades where faith languishes. It is a fellowship that is not an institution. It does not possess the quality of self-perpetuation by the authority of ordination or the laws of succession. When faith ends this community ends. But Christ can create this community out of nothing, through faith.

The community that belongs to Christ and his new covenant is therefore not a legally organized religious institution. Its order is not based on a system of perpetual ordinations, and its government does not consist of a succession of hierarchs. It is a fellowship that has no parallels. Its unique character comes from its unique Lord.

God sent Jesus into the world not to found a new "historical religion," but to create a new covenant in which the risen Christ would stand as the new link between man and God, in the place of all merely cultic and legalistic religion. It is primarily as an

---

* cf Isaiah 42:6

invisible but living teacher of righteousness that we come to know Jesus as the mediator of the new covenant and the orderer of God's new covenant people. If there had been no cross and no resurrection, there would have been no new community.

Jesus did not come to found an institution that would carry on after he was gone, but he came to die and rise again and continue to be present in the midst of his people as their abiding head. This explains why during his lifetime he is so casual about the community and its structure, even though his disciples were pressing him to be more specific. This means that such concepts as "founding fathers," "mother church," "apostolic succession," "rites based on perpetual ordinances," "authoritative scriptures as the basis of church law," are all alien to the spirit that pervades the new covenant. The new community is of such a nature that historical continuity and an unbroken succession of leaders are not relevant to its life.

The Strategy of Renewal

When the church declines or disappears from the historical scene, the problem of renewal is not a problem of restoring a link with some period in the historical past which is regarded as normative. The path of renewal in the day of the new covenant leads directly to Christ who is the new covenant. As men turn to Christ the light, they will be formed into a community—the children of light. Therefore leading people to Christ is the strategy of renewal that belongs to the new covenant. This is a strategy that is as free as possible from the spirit of primitivism. The words, "Jerusalem which is above is your mother," were frequently quoted by Fox, and he believed that the wise seeker for the renewal of the church will look above and not backward for the answers he seeks.

This does not mean that the Bible tells us nothing about Christian community, or that there is any special virtue in being ignorant of church history. It means rather that we must use the Bible, history, and tradition as people who know that the redemptive community of which Christ is the head is rooted and grounded in faith and cannot be separated from faith. It cannot be rediscovered and reconstructed by the most careful biblical exegesis and the most exhaustive knowledge of church history. The Bible is not an encyclopedia of religious knowledge; it is the book which testifies of Christ, that is, leads us to him. He is the substance of that to which the whole Bible bears witness. To use the Bible as if it were itself the eternal word is to mistake the purpose for which it was given. Jesus says, "You search the Scriptures and it is they that bear witness to me; yet you refuse to come to me"*

Church Government and Order

For Fox there is but one root and ground that can serve as the basis for church government and order, and this is the dynamic, personal, "we–thou" relationship between God's people and God's son. The living Christ is the "living foundation"[3] and "living Mediator"[4] who orders and governs God's people in the new covenant.

Fox always assumes that preaching the gospel produces community. He says in his Journal, "As everyone hath received Christ Jesus the Lord, so walk in him and let him be their Lord and Orderer. For the preaching of the gospel of Christ Jesus is to the intent that all may come to be ... heirs of Christ and of his government."[5] His own object as an evangelist was to leave people "unto the Lord Jesus Christ's teaching and ordering."[6] He says that God first sent him forth "to declare the everlasting gospel, and then after people had received the gospel, I was moved to go through the nation, to advise them to set up ... meetings ... And this was the end, that all who had received ... Christ Jesus, might ... possess ... his government in the church ... And so ... being heirs of Christ they are heirs of him, and of his government; ... heirs of the order of the gospel, which is from heaven, and not by man nor of man."[7]

In the days of the new covenant of light, says Fox, "all flesh must come to the spirit of God, and be led and guided by it, if they will see Christ's heavenly spiritual government and order..."[8]

Fox maintains that God's people in the new covenant are ordered in a special way. This ordering under the gospel is of a different nature from all human devices for ordering, governing, and giving cohesion to human society. The church of Jesus Christ

---

* cf. John 5:39/40

is not something which has naturally evolved in human history. This gospel and the order of it "is not of man, nor by man, neither is it received but by the revelation of Jesus Christ, sent down from heaven."[9] "The Gospel is from heaven," says Fox, "here is eternal fellowship and order [and] here is our order."[10]

The order of the gospel fellowship is not determined by the ordinances of the "founder" during his lifetime, but it is determined by what Christ does *now*. Everything that gives form and structure and order to the new covenant community is the consequence of the action of Christ. He is at the center of this community, and it is what he does that causes the community to appear and determines its form. His action is experienced by the community in three ways. First, as he is present in the midst of the *gathered* community, teaching, instructing, and guiding them. His people can hear his voice as he raises up spokesmen and sends his spirit by which the spoken word is confirmed in the heart of each member. Fox says, "they that do obey the voice of ... Christ Jesus in his light ... they know the order of Christ."[11] Second, he speaks to the individual member and shows him how to cultivate his gifts and offer them acceptably toward the harmonious functioning of the whole community. Every member is called to contribute something, and the functioning of the community is dependent on the faithful response of each member to the call of Christ. And third, God and Christ send the spirit which is good and holy, and which helps us to know Christ as the one head of God's people, and helps us to hear him and obey him.

This community is not like any other community. Christ is the author of it. It is not man-made. Just as the gospel that proclaims the Christ event is a *new thing*, so this ordered community that belongs to the gospel is a new thing. By this gospel and the order that belongs to it, God has created the fullest possible means of experiencing community. It is this kind of community, based on hearing and obeying the living God, that is man's true habitation. It is the spiritual home that God intended for man in creating him.

This is the *ground* and *root* of the early Quaker understanding of Christian community and church order. It is the approach that underlies the Quaker conception of ministry, worship, discipline, pastoral care, missionary activity, and everything else.

In 1671 Fox wrote to Friends in Carolina, "Keep your meetings and meet together in the name of Jesus ... and you gathering in his name ... he is your prophet, your shepherd, your bishop, your priest, in the midst of you, to open you, to sanctify you ... and to quicken you with life; wait in his power and light, that you may be children of the light, by believing in the light, which is the life in Christ; that you may be grafted into him, the true root, and built upon him, the true foundation..."[12]

We must remember that when Fox said that "Christ is your foundation ... to build upon,"[13] he saw this foundation as a dynamic relationship to a living being. The new covenant community exists only where the master-disciple relationship to the living Christ is experienced. On several occasions Fox concluded his account of the establishment of new meetings with the statement that Friends "were settled in the new covenant Christ Jesus, and built upon him their rock and foundation."[14]

Religious institutions do not take as their foundation a personal relationship. The institution-makers want more security. Fox compares the spirit of the institution-makers to the spirit "that led Nimrod to build Babel, a city to preserve him and them after the flood, but God did confound them and their work. And so he will do all such builders. For you see how God did confound all the Jewish builders, yes, the wise master builders, who rejected Christ the cornerstone, and his order, and his government, and his counsel."[15] This basic master-disciple relationship to the living Christ is the chief cornerstone, or top stone, that all institution makers reject.

Penington says that the sign by which the church is known and "which distinguisheth her from all other assemblies and gatherings" is "the nature, life and presence of the head with her and in her. This none hath but the true church, the gathered body..."[16] When Fox speaks of "the church in God of which Christ is the head," it is this unique community that he has in mind. Fox observes that Christ was known as the head of the church in the apostolic age, after he was crucified and risen from the dead, "and so he is still to all true Christians" and "is the present head of the church."[17]

The Authority In The Gospel

There is no debate among the early Quakers as to whether the seat of authority is in the Scriptures, or in the hierarchical leadership, or in synods, or in church tradition. "The authority is in the gospel which is the power of God, and which is not of man nor by man, but of God and from Christ."[18]

Fox believed the gospel releases God's power in an evil world. And what is this gospel? It is that Christ has "come to reign, and has set up his kingdom in power and authority, and majesty."[19] Fox says, "...feel Christ's reign and authority, in which you may all act in his power and authority."[20] "Here is the authority of our men's and women's meetings and other meetings in the name of Jesus, the gospel of Christ, the power of God, which is not of man nor by man ... but from heaven received by the holy Ghost."[21] "For amongst us Christ is King ... we look not at persons, but at the power of God; and know the reign of Christ amongst us."[22]

The gospel which is the power of God is the authority for the people of God in the new covenant, but Fox also lays special emphasis on the cross of Christ as the place where God's power is manifested. He says, "There hath been an apostasy in the whole of Christendom from the cross of Christ the power of God,"[23] and he expects that the restored church of the new covenant will be a church of the cross. He says that the true Christian fellowship is in the cross of Christ which is the power of God.[24] If all Christendom had submitted to the yoke of the cross then they would have had a fellowship in the cross of Christ."[25] "...in the power of God is the fellowship of the cross, which keeps over all the fellowships of the world and crucifies them."[26] "...the cross of Christ is the everlasting power of God: so no longer do you keep in fellowship, but as you keep in the cross of Christ."[27]

The Call to Community

There is a widespread notion in the present Society of Friends that the Quaker community owed its beginning to a chain of unforeseen circumstances, and that there is nothing in Fox's message that leads inevitably to the formation of community.

Chapter III

Rufus Jones says, "The early Society of Friends ... was a creation of unconscious insight, of unpremeditated intention."[28] This note has been struck by at least half a dozen modern Quaker writers who should have known better. It is hard to understand how anyone could fail to see that the call to community is an integral part of Fox's message. Fox himself maintained that his message was misunderstood unless the social side of it was taken seriously. He says, "All that receive this gospel, the power of God unto salvation, in their hearts, receive Christ (the power of God), and his government and order in the power. And Christ reigns in their hearts in his power; and such come into the gospel order ... And this gospel which is the power of God ... keeps all that believe in it, in the everlasting ... order ... So in this gospel they are established in the order of it ... Now all they that do not receive the gospel of Christ, the power of God to salvation ... such are blind concerning the order of the gospel."[29] But even those who have received Christ will not recognize "Christ's heavenly spiritual government and order" without the help of the spirit of God. Fox says that those who profess that Christ is come but who vex and quench his spirit "are not like to receive Christ into their hearts, nor come into his heavenly order and established peaceable government ... For it is God that gives the heavenly understanding of Christ's established government and order. And they that quench and vex the spirit of God, will rebel against Christ's established government and order."[30]

Fox's teaching concerning the gospel order occupies a very large part of his writings. It is the part of his teaching that aroused most opposition both inside and outside the Quaker fellowship.

But, in spite of all opposition from within and without, the gospel order was established and Fox could say four years before his death, "The Lord God with his spirit sealed to you, that your meetings are of his ordering and gathering and he hath owned them by honoring you with his blessed presence ... He hath sealed your meetings by his Spirit to you and that your gathering hath been by the Lord to Christ his Son, and in his name: and not by man."[31]

The Quaker missioners and evangelists proclaimed that the Christian community was being given a new order—the order that belongs to the gospel—and that the old order must be totally rejected. They were not content to make this proclamation in a passive manner. They believed that they were required to make this proclamation in a way that challenged the existing order and called all men and women to come out of it.

The Victory of the Lamb

The tension between the Quakers and established Christian groups was not because of some *particular* difference or differences. The Quakers were laying the axe to the root of all institutional Christianity. They identified themselves with the saints who, in the book of Revelation, war on the side of the Lamb against "mystery Babylon," which is the false church. Fox says that this false church has "whored ... from the new and living way, Christ Jesus: [and] from the spirit of God into false religions, ways and worship."[32] "But now is Christ come, who will make war in righteousness, and destroy with the sword of his mouth all these inventors and inventions that have ... been set up since the days of the apostles."[33] "The wrath of the Lord is risen upon all ... who are gathered in the apostasy ... from the prophets' life, the apostles' life ... from the life of my apostles, of my prophets have you been all scattered and apostatized and so true ministry hath been lost, true apostles' life lost, true prophets' life lost ... amongst whom are so many names ... setting up your inventions but inwardly ... apostatized. But ... the Lamb will have the victory and ... the throne and the sceptre that is everlasting is come and witnessed and set over the world ... and all gatherings ... from that shall be broken."[34] "Since the days of the apostles ... false ministers and this false church got up and spread over the world ... but the Lamb and the saints shall have the victory ... [and] this false woman, mystery Babylon, shall be confounded and the true church known again."[35]

The affirmation, "the Lamb and the saints shall have the victory," is repeated at least fifteen times in Fox's writings, and he reminds the Quaker missioners, "...many walls and troops have ye gone through and leaped over, and the Lord hath given you dominion over that which warred against you; and by the power of the Lord ye have overcome and in the power of the Lord ye will overcome all..."³⁶

The early Quaker was a man of war, and in Fox's vision the people of God in the new covenant are a people "undaunted and valiant for Christ Jesus and God's name ... upon the earth."³⁷ He exhorts Friends to "know a kingdom which hath no end and fight for that with spiritual weapons ... gather men to war, as many as you can, and set up as many as you can with these weapons."³⁸

In his recent book, *The Quakers in Puritan England*, Hugh Barbour has directed our attention to the importance of "the Lamb's war" in early Quaker experience, and he quite rightly points out that for the Puritan also, the Christian life was a life of warfare. He endeavors to show that spiritual warfare as Quakers knew it was a particular manifestation of the spiritual war in which the whole Puritan world was engaged.

There is a measure of truth in this. For the Puritan the enemy was the world, the flesh, and the devil. The world was a great battlefield in the conflict between Christ and Satan. The Christian was involved in the increasing war of the spiritual man against the carnal man. The Quakers were involved in this war too. They believed that Christ had come to destroy the devil and his works, and they fought against those corrupt social institutions that they believed to be the work of the devil. They expected that everything that has been spoiled and corrupted by disobedience would be restored again by Christ and his saints. The Puritan and the Quaker were both at war with society as it is organized apart from the wisdom and authority of God. They both called this godless society, Babylon, the city of confusion. Babylon is the enemy.

The True Church and the False

But this is not the whole story. For the Quakers there is another Babylon with which they are at war. This is what the Book of Revelation calls "mystery Babylon" or the false church. In the war in which early Friends were engaged the opponent was most usually the institutional church. When Fox says, "the Lamb and the saints shall have the victory," the victory that he has in mind is the victory of the true non-institutional church over the false institutional church.

The Puritan also read Revelation and was also at war with the false church. But in both his war with the corrupt institutions of worldly society, and his war with the false church, the Puritan differed from the Quaker in his basic strategy and in his understanding of the issues. In its battle against worldly evil, the Puritan ideal was rooted in a vision of national "uniformity based upon the will of a godly people and maintained with the support of a godly civil state."[39] Although the Quakers were willing to crusade for just laws and a right administration of justice, they saw the "new earth" that would be restored by Christ as coming as the result of obedience and cross-bearing, rather than by means of political success. When the Quakers found themselves in a dominant position politically they did not choose to impose their ideal of corporate righteousness on the whole community by the power of the magistrate.

But it is in their conception of the false church, and their vision of the true church, that the Puritans are most widely separated from the Quakers. For the Puritan, the Bible is the ultimate criterion of church order. The false church is that church which fails to conform to the biblical standard as Puritans defined it. The true church is, conversely, the church which does conform to these standards. Consequently, the Puritan war against the false church is a reformers' war. It submits its lists of reforms after the manner of an ultimatum. Its war aims are defined in its lists of reforms.

The Quaker attack on the false church proceeds from an entirely different ground and root. It is based on the basic presupposition that God sent Christ to be a new and living way to God, and that the people of God in the new covenant would be gathered to Christ through the prophetic experience of hearing and obeying.

Perhaps, of all the Quakers, Isaac Penington was most cognizant of the wide gulf that separated the Puritan and the Quaker conceptions of the true church in God and the false church which is of man's making. Penington had fought this war on both the Puritan and the Quaker fronts, and he saw their objectives as being so different that there was no possibility of thinking of them as allies. "I have smarted deeply for these things," he confesses. "For [as a Puritan] I also did believe and expect great things in a church-state and way of worship ... and was not without ... experiences there. But all this the Lord broke down by a strong hand."[40] He says of his former Puritan colleagues: "They cry up practices in religion; duties, ordinances, the means, the means; a church, a church ... but they find the church before they have found the spirit of the Lord, and so they find not the church that is in God, the church that is of his building..."[41]

To the Puritan, John Norton, he says, "Your church, your ministry, your order and government, your whole way of teaching and worship is not of God ... but an invention and imitation, set up in the way of resemblance of what once was truly so."[42] In a book directed against "all error from the life, among both Papists and Protestants," he says, "The ground wherein men's religion grows (even the most zealous) is bad; ... which stands in the understanding and will of man, rearing up a pleasant building there, but keeps from the life and building in it. But the true religion stands in receiving a principle of life; which, by its growth forms a vessel for itself..."[43] (italics mine). He speaks of the religiosity "which is so busy in the willing and running and makes such a noise about duties, and ordinances, and graces," and he speaks of "the seed of life which is the heir, which lies underneath all this and must remain slain while this lives": but, he says, "if ever you hear the voice of the Son of God, this will live and the other die."[44] It is an either–or proposition, and Penington declares: "There are but these two: and he that is joined to the one of these, is not joined to the other."[45]

"But Ye Must Come Out Of It All"

Therefore the call of early Friends is not to accept a catalogue of particular reforms, but to begin again from another ground and root and to rebuild from the foundation. Penington says, "To come out of one part of Babylonish worship, that is not enough; or to come out of some pieces of Babylonish knowledge and wisdom, will not answer the call; but ye must come out of it all."[46] The Lamb's war, as the Quakers saw it, was not a contest between two types of institutional Christianity, but a fight to the finish between institutional Christianity and non-institutional Christianity. For George Fox, the Quaker movement was a genuine breakthrough for the cause of non-institutional Christianity. He says that when a man "hath seen all the religions of man's making and is come out of them ... what a noise then do the religion makers make ... when they have broken through the wall of their city and religion."[47] Are there not signs that the time is again ripe for a movement that will break through the walled city of man-made religion?

Chapter IV

Catholic Quakerism and the Ecumenical Movement*

If the Society of Friends fails to recover the comprehensive vision of Christianity which is its true heritage, then the force most likely to determine its character and destiny in the 20th century is the Ecumenical Movement. And so it seems necessary and right to discuss the relation of the Ecumenical Movement to that comprehensive vision of Christianity that I have been calling Catholic Quakerism.

But at once we are faced with a major difficulty. Although the Ecumenical Movement has existed for about fifty years, and has produced a vast literature, it is still very difficult to define it for purposes of discussion. For some, it is the great movement for reunification after four centuries of dispersion. For others it has absolutely nothing to do with reunification. For some it is to be understood in terms of the statements that have emerged from its great conferences. For others, its true meaning must be seen in the light of recent trends and the possible outcome of those trends if they continue to develop. The friends and well-wishers of the Ecumenical Movement all seem to have their own personal understanding of its meaning and significance, and to react violently to any image of the movement but their own.

One thing, at least, we can say: before the appearance of the Ecumenical Movement the denominations did not seriously converse with each other through regular channels of communication, and now they do. I see nothing in the concept of Catholic Quakerism to prevent Quakers from participating in these conversations.

*The situation that some Quakers find themselves in today is more inclusive and open-ended.

Catholic Quakerism and the Ecumenical Movement

In what follows, I wish to explore some of the implications that would have to be considered if Quakers were to accept the vision of Catholic Quakerism as the basis for their role in ecumenical conversation. I will begin by mentioning some recent trends in the Ecumenical Movement, and then proceed to examine some of the presuppositions that are generally accepted as the basis for current ecumenical discussion, and, finally, I will attempt to evaluate the vision of Christian renewal that is emerging in ecumenical circles and compare it with the vision of Christian renewal that belongs to Catholic Quakerism.

A New Approach

It seems to be generally agreed that the Third World Conference on Faith and Order at Lund (in 1952) marked a turning point in the Faith and Order Movement. Before Lund, the procedure had been to analyze and compare different positions at issue among the churches which stood in the way of Christian unity[1]. This revealed that there was a great deal more agreement than had been supposed, and this led to a period of optimism. But, says Albert C. Outler, "This first approach—the method of comparative agreement—works well enough until it reaches the hard core of residual *dis*agreement."[2] "As things now stand," says Outler, "our existing disagreements on the doctrines of church, ministry, and sacraments are 'insoluble'."[3] The churches seemed to have gone as far as they could along the path of comparative ecclesiology, and so at Lund there was the beginning of a new approach in which the churches would together "study Christ and the relation of Christ to His Church and draw the consequences for the doctrine of the Church."[4]

Taken at its face value, this approach comes very close to George Fox's approach. There are some Quakers who feel that as long as ecumenical thinking keeps headed in this direction it will inevitably lead to a rediscovery of the early Quaker vision. If this new approach were taken absolutely seriously it would undoubtedly lead to a rediscovery of that other "root and ground" that was the foundation of the Quaker movement 300 years ago.

But the ecumenical quest is being carried forward within two self-imposed limitations that will tend to prevent the rediscovery of the Quaker vision. The first of these two limitations is the assumption that the church of Jesus Christ must have an institutional structure. This means, on the one hand, that the quest for the experience of the *koinonia*—the fellowship of common life in the spirit—takes the form of a quest for the church as a spiritual organism. This is only one side of the church's life, however. Its other side is the institutional side. The problem is how to keep the spiritual and institutional in balance, for it is assumed that the institutional side is just as much needed as the spiritual side.

I want to examine this assumption. But first it will be necessary to try to define what is meant by *institution* and *institutional*. In its broadest meaning any social organization that has had a definite beginning in time by a definite act of institution can be called an institution. But it will be necessary to get a sharper definition than this, because what is being discussed as the non-institutional side of the church also had a definite beginning through a definite act of institution. Perhaps we can best pin down the meaning of the institutional church by describing its function. It is that side or function of the church's life that standardizes faith and practice and guarantees the church's perpetuity.

Sociology defines an institution as a definite and established structure, built around and sustaining one or more specific functions.[5] The functions of the institutional church are to insure uniformity of faith and practice, and to guarantee perpetuity. The reason why so much importance is attached to the institutional church is that it is seen as the only means of maintaining uniform order and genuine continuity. I am going to try to discuss the institutional church in terms of these two functions.

In *The Old and the New in the Church*, we are told that "economic order, government, family, communication, art and religion" all have their "institutional structure and organization.[6] Gustafson claims that "similarities exist between the Christian community and the state, the nation, voluntary associations for charitable purposes and many other groups and movements. There may be an irreducible uniqueness, a differentium that distinguishes the church from all historical communities, but this does not make it absolutely different in kind."[7]

All institutions must have some kind of constitution and rules for the succession of a hierarchy. In the Christian church these are furnished by the "three essential and enduring dominical institutions: the Gospel (word), the Sacraments, and the Ministry ... through which these are administered."[8] So much for the sociology of the institutional church.

On the theological side, we have a number of theological explanations. Perhaps the simplest theological apology for the institutional church is the one that simply states that God sent Jesus into the world to establish a religious institution, which he accomplished by instituting certain perpetual ordinances and by appointing twelve hierarchs whose successors govern the church in perpetuity.

But the theological approach is not always that simple. Brunner says, "The nature of the Christian brotherhood is basically different from the nature of an institution..."[9] He describes this brotherhood as "a thoroughly uncultic, unsacred, spiritual brotherhood, which lives in trusting obedience to its Lord Christ and in the love to the brethren which He bestows, and knows itself as the Body of Christ through the Holy Spirit which dwells in it."[10] The social character of this brotherhood is determined by its spiritual character.[11] "Sociologically the Ekklesia would have to be defined as a fellowship in the most authentic sense, in distinction from an association."[12] Fellowship, he says, "differs from association precisely in that it has its goal in itself and is not there to serve a further end."[13]

But for Brunner the decisive thing about the church in our day is that the Holy Spirit was inexplicably withdrawn in the first century, and we are now compelled to get along with an institutional church which can be inspired by the non-institutional church of the first century, but cannot imitate it. "The institutional form," he says, "does not belong to the essence of the Ekklesia. But as we men are constituted this is necessary as its covering, its shell, and its instrument."[14]

Hendrik Kraemer's position on the institutional church has some points in common with Brunner's. He says, "...true as it may be that for many important historical reasons the church has become from a charismatic fellowship an institutional

Chapter IV

Church, she must acknowledge that, as to her *nature*, she is always charismatic, for she is the working field of the Holy Spirit. Her being an institution is a human necessity but not the nature of the Church."[15]

So here are two theological views: one sees the church as a divinely given institution and the other sees it, as it was originally given by God, as a non-institutional fellowship, or brotherhood, which has degenerated into an institution because of the vagaries of the spirit, or because of human weakness and necessity.

There is a third theological view which I find to be most commonly held by those who have contributed to the ecumenical conversations. This is the view that the church is a combination of institutional and non-institutional elements, and that from the beginning it has been this way by divine intention, and that any other view is heretical. The exponents for this view believe that the doctrine of the incarnation demands that we see the church as a combination of the divine and the human. It has a heavenly and spiritual body: the *koinonia*, which is the fellowship in the spirit, and also the historical, human institution, which is the "official church body." If the church must have a human body as well as a spiritual body, what could be more human than a human institution? This doctrine claims as its basis the ancient orthodox doctrine of the incarnation, and its exponents are prepared to hurl the charge of ecclesiastical docetism against those who are not prepared to accept this doctrine. In *Faith and Order Findings*, 1963, this statement appears: "As the incarnate Son was truly man, so is the Church wrought out of the stuff of human existence. The Church is shaped in and out by the realities of human historicity and sociality. Therefore, the Church is not some 'ideal' community, existing in airy abstraction from the affairs of men. Neither is it 'spiritual' in the sense that it is to be contrasted with the hard and inevitable materialities of that world of history and sociality. To call the Church ideal or spiritual in those senses is to fall into ecclesiological docetism akin to the ancient heresy which denied to our Lord his physical body."[16] In *The Old and the New in the Church*, a Faith and Order publication, it is asserted that it is a misconception "to posit a dichotomy or even an opposition between the free and unfettered fellowship of Christian believers and ecclesiastical structures." This tendency is usually accompanied by "a spiritualizing interpretation of the New Testament evidence, according to which the *koinonia* of the Spirit was a strictly personal fellowship in faith and love, uncontaminated by any institutional features." The report calls this latter view "ecclesiological docetism."[17]

Now the element in this doctrine that needs further critical study is the assertion that the institutional factor in the historic church is built into the Gospel and new covenant and that to question it is tantamount to denying the physical existence of Jesus Christ. We must, first of all, strongly affirm that the church must have a visible, outward, gathered life in which there is social cohesion and historical existence. The spiritualizers are wrong. The true church is not the invisible church. God intends his new covenant people to be an objective community in history. But the question at issue here is whether the church can have true objective historical existence without being a human institution. Can the church only achieve outward, objective, historical existence by accepting the role and character of a human institution? In asserting that this is the only alternative to a spiritualized interpretation, and in claiming that all dissenters from this view are heretics, a limitation is being imposed on ecumenical discussion.

I wish to maintain that in the Quaker vision as George Fox understood it, we have a counter claim that the church can have social cohesion, and a real, outward, objective existence in history, without being a human institution.

Tradition and the Traditions

The second great limitation on ecumenical discussion is related to what is being discussed under the category of the Tradition and the traditions. In its main outlines, this discussion assumes that there is one overarching Christian tradition which is the matrix of all particular Christian traditions, and that this overarching tradition has the quality of wholeness, whereas each particular denominational tradition is partial and fragmentary.

Chapter IV

What is being said about the wholeness of the one overarching tradition is not always as clear as what is being said about the fragmentary nature of the several particular traditions. But Albert C. Outler has produced a statement that could probably win a wide range of assent. He says, *"Jesus Christ is the Christian dogma.* Everything else in Christian thought derives from or subserves this primordial conviction. And the Christian tradition has, as its sole function, to bring men into living encounter with Jesus Christ as He truly was and is, and to bring them together in His Body, the church."[18] This is something to which George Fox could have subscribed. But immediately we are told that this overarching tradition includes the proposition that the New Testament is the sole and sufficient rule of faith and practice.[19] "For each and for all," says Outler, "the Word of God in Scripture is the constitutive tradition of the Christian community ... The New Testament is therefore the primary locus of the Christian tradition. Having produced it and having acknowledged it as authoritative by canonizing it, the Church thereafter bound itself to the New Testament as its charter."[20]

And in *Faith and Order Trends (Vol. 3, No. 4)* we are told that the church was "founded to proclaim God's saving act ... to be continually used by the Spirit to make Christ present again and again through the proclamation of the word and the administration of the Sacraments. Through these means Christ is always at work through his Spirit ... Since God's presence is made real to us through [these] instituted means, there must be no playing of charisma and institution against one another."[21]

It seems plain that when the great tradition leaves the realm of generalities, and begins to be spelled out in particular terms, the pattern that emerges is one that is very familiar to anyone who is acquainted with the Protestant tradition as it has been developing since the 16th century in English, Germanic, and Scandinavian speaking lands. But this pattern excludes Quakerism as George Fox understood it. The Catholic Quakerism of George Fox* is not a part of this tradition.

With respect to the concept of the many traditions, ecumenical thought seems to be united in the belief that all of them, with-

*see footnote p. 1.

out exception, are partial and fragmentary. This sweeping judgment is not made on the basis of a study of the content of each separate tradition. It is an a priori judgment that includes them all. Furthermore, it is shocking to the ecumenical mind whenever the claim is made that a particular Christian tradition has the quality of wholeness about it.[22] Outler says that those who make such a claim are odious, stubborn, confused, self-sufficient, competitive, reactionary, smug, self-righteous, bigoted, impatient, tendentious, self-centered, separatist, condescending, acrimonious, intransigent, and piously truculent. One might have expected a more open attitude from a writer who has borne down rather heavily on the unfairness of some polemical theologians.

To study Christ and let Christ order his church, and to lead people to Christ and bring them together in his body, the church, is a program in which all Christians can participate. *Solus Christus* can be the word that binds all together and heals all wounds. But are we making "Christ alone" the basis of ecumenical conversation if these conversations presuppose that the institutional question, the sacramental question, and the question of the authority of scriptures have already been disposed of because all participants have accepted a certain overarching tradition in which these questions are dealt with in a certain way? Oliver Tomkins has recently made the statement that "unity is essentially a common faith, grounded in Scripture and testified to in creed and liturgy, a common acceptance of the two sacraments of the Lord's ordinance and a common ministry whose grace and authority are accepted throughout the fellowship."[23]

If these assumptions about unity are held by most participants in the ecumenical movement, as I believe to be the case, it weakens the claim of the World Council Central Committee (1950) that "The World Council ... does not prejudge the ecclesiological problem."[24]

The general statement that "Christ alone" is the basis for ecumenical conversation has an appeal that few true Christians can resist. But behind this general statement are certain ever-present assumptions. If the Society of Friends is to participate in ecumenical dialogue it must either accept these assumptions or challenge them. I maintain that if Quakers are to be true to their own highest vision and historic mission they must challenge these assumptions.

Christian Renewal

At the 1964 Conference in Nottingham the ecumenical task was described as operating in three spheres, namely: unity, renewal, and mission. Renewal is a major concern of the ecumenical movement, and there is wide acceptance of the view that unity without renewal would be hardly worth working for. Therefore the ecumenical movement sees that whatever significant gains are made in the effort toward Christian renewal are related to its work. I want here to comment on the character of some contemporary efforts toward Christian renewal, and to compare them with the vision of renewal that belongs to Catholic Quakerism.

It appears that the patterns of renewal that have been emerging fall into three major categories. They are either concerned with remodeling the role of the clergy, or reviving the laity, or mending broken relations between clergy and laity.

Within each of these major categories several patterns of renewal have developed. In the last category mentioned, we are dealing with a situation in which clergy and people have drifted apart, especially in industrialized urban societies. This is noticeable in countries with a state church tradition where there are vast numbers of baptized "Christians" who seldom or never assemble to hear the word preached or receive the sacraments. Among the devices for bringing priest and people together are the House Church Movement, the Iona Community, and the Worker Priests. In Chicago and Harlem, teams of clergymen from various denominations co-operate to tackle the social and religious problems of the inner city in a movement that has been called "Parish Life Renewal." "Chaplains in Industry" represents another attempt to bring the clergyman to the people.

Most of these movements have been initiated by the clergy, and the clergyman has the key role in most of them. It is inevitable that they should have come into existence, for the obvious reason that no honest clergyman can simply accept a situation in which he has no contact with large numbers of souls who are supposed to be under his care.

Essentially, all these devices are schemes to bring the old clergy system up to date and make it better adapted to the present religious and social situation. This is certainly a kind of renewal, but I cannot see how it can be related to George Fox's vision of the church reborn.

The Role of the Clergy

In America there is another type of renewal which has attempted to re-evaluate and re-define the role of the "minister of the congregation." Two factors have been at work to bring changes in this area. First is the intolerable position into which the minister was thrust as a result of trends in the organizational side of the American denomination. Responsibility for the local congregation became concentrated in the "minister of the congregation," and he became the full-time promoter of "a successful church program" which seemed always to be leading him into a way of life ever more remote from his original calling. The number of people preparing for pastoral work in a local congregation is steadily decreasing in the theological seminaries. A radical break with traditional concepts of the minister's role was long overdue.

Another factor was the new interest in the role of the laity in the life of the church. In the early days of the ecumenical movement it consisted of a dialogue almost entirely limited to clergymen. There has been an increasing concern about this one-sidedness in the church's life. The new emphasis on the importance of the laity has caused the minister to think of himself primarily as an organizer and co-ordinator of lay activity. His job is to combat passivity among the laity and to promote social responsibility. In the larger congregations, the ordained minister becomes one of the members of a leadership team that consists of several ordained or unordained professionals. It is possible that some denominations may discontinue ordination, and there is discussion about the propriety of the title "Reverend." But all these changes are not likely to reduce the number of professionally trained workers in the church. In most congregations the minister will remain the one professional in a community of non-professionals. Congregational life without the professionally trained leader at its center is hard for most Christians to envisage, and this may be largely because they have never heard of any alternative to this pattern. However drastically his role is reconceived, the professionally trained minister will still have a job in the institutional church of the future.

George Fox's vision of the church reborn had absolutely no place in it for this kind of leadership. Catholic Quakerism offers a real alternative to the clergy-laity pattern of church order.

Lay Responsibility

The third category of renewal is to be found in the new efforts to develop lay responsibility and to conceive of the role of the layman as a special Christian vocation. This development began to make its appearance in the Oxford Conference of 1937, and at Evanston in 1954 a "Department of the Laity" was included in the structure of the World Council of Churches. In this category also there is a constellation of methods and techniques that are designed to bring about a rebirth of the laity. An important feature of this development is the Lay Center or Lay Academy, which is often a conference center but sometimes appears as a settled community. There are at least twenty-five such centers in the United States and forty or more in Europe. Some of these have a Retreat program, but the Retreat Movement, which is allied to Lay Centers, is not always associated with some particular center or centers. Another conspicuous feature in the movement for renewal is the Small Group or Cell Group. There are few large congregations in the United States which do not rely heavily on this technique to give the average church member a sense of close fellowship, and an opportunity to participate in the life of a group of manageable size. The fact that small groups develop a keener sense of fellowship than large groups seems to have been one of the great ecclesiological discoveries of the 20th century.

The drive toward success in terms of bigness has led the suburban church to a situation in which congregational life becomes impersonal and the activities of the church become over-institutionalized. It has never seemed to occur to anyone that congregations might be made smaller. The support of from one to five or six professionally trained leaders presupposes a large supporting community. To house a large congregation in harmony with traditional ideas of church architecture, plus facilities for a modern conception of a church program, takes a large capital outlay and the assurance of continued support. The institutional church has certain standards of success, and these standards cannot be met if church enrollment falls below a certain level. A certain degree of bigness is essential to the life of the institutionalized church. But the disadvantages of bigness can be offset by making use of this wonderful new ecclesiological discovery—the small group.

Howard Grimes says that, "Perhaps there is no solution to the problem of the large congregation except one which involves some sort of structure that makes possible maximum discussion of important issues in face to face groups…" He maintains that "each congregation ought to have as many small groups as possible. If they are properly used each will become something of a 'buzz group' within the congregation. This means, of course, that there must be some method of 'feedback' from the small groups to 'the official body of the church'"[25] This passage indicates that these groups are quite unofficial, which means that they are really not an integral part of the church structure at all. They have many forms, and their life span may be long or short. They may be either clergy-initiated or lay-initiated. Some small groups are exclusively devotional in character. Others are task centred or project centered. The most common form perhaps is the "study group." Study groups are supposed to focus in two fields: "biblical faith" and "the human situation."[26] It is important that groups should range from twelve to twenty, that they should have lay leadership, and that all members should participate as fully as possible.

There is no question that the small group does furnish the means for face to face discussions, wider participation, and closer fellowship. And it might further be conceded that the development of such small groups will help the large congregations to survive. But it is surely extravagant to maintain that this "small-groups-plus-the-big-group" combination is in fact a revolutionary new concept of the nature of the church, or that the kind of renewal that results from the use of the small group method is, in fact, a rediscovery and re-application of the power of the gospel.

The gospel has fellowship-forming power, but, as long as we rely on group dynamics to make up for the lack of fellowship in the institutional church, we are postponing the day when the real *koinonia* of the spirit will become a reality through the power of the gospel.

The small group may be primarily or exclusively for laymen, but it is a product of the clerical mind. For the clerical mind the first step is to get an "official church body" and then somehow infuse it with a sense of close fellowship and lay responsibility. But is this not looking at the problem the wrong way round? In the Quaker vision the church *is* the *laos* and the church *is* the *koinonia*. *Laos* and *koinonia* are not accessories of a church which claims "official" status without them. *Without laos and koinonia there is no church at all.* This is why the Quakers have developed no literature on the laity or on fellowship as subjects of special interest.

Lay Vocation

Another line that has been pursued by those in quest of Christian renewal is the emphasis being placed on lay Christianity as a vocation to compensate for the over-emphasis that has been put on the vocation of the clergyman. Fox did not believe that the church consists of laymen and non-laymen, and he did not believe that some Christians are called to be laymen while other Christians have some other calling. It is a mistake to think that it is the special vocation of some Christians to be laymen. In the New Covenant church the category of "the people" does not stand over against some other category of Christian, such as priest or clergy. There is only one who stands over against God's people as prophet, priest, and king, and this is Christ himself.

In the only place that I have found where Fox uses the word "lay" it is to point out that Paul never called the churches "laypeople," but he addressed them as "brethren."[27] In over fifty instances Fox addresses Friends Meetings as "brethren." He says of those who have been called to the ministry, "...keep the ministers equal brethren."[28] Fox never uses the term "priesthood of all believers" as far as I know, but he says, "Christ ... maketh priests of all his church,"[29] and "Christ ... makes all his believers priests."

I believe that all dreams of the rebirth of lay Christianity are doomed as long as the layman is regarded as a Christian with a special calling, and as long as it is believed that some Christians are not called to be laymen.[30]

Fox believed that in the New Covenant church the category of priest had been abolished once for all. The Catholic and Protestant traditions have no real alternative to the clergy system and, consequently, the quest for the rebirth of the laity within these traditions must be, and is, a quest for the role of the laity in a church that does not consist entirely of laymen. In his book, *A Theology for the Laity*, Hendrik Kraemer says, "...the ordained ministry ... have indeed their important place and function"[31] and the Evanston Report on the Laity states: "Clergy and laity belong together in the Church; if the Church is to perform her mission in the world, they need each other."[32] Congar, the Roman Catholic writer, says in his book on *Lay People in the Church* that "lay people will always be a subordinate order in the church."[33]

Of these three types or categories of renewal, the first two are concerned with remodelling the clergy and with methods for bringing clergy and laity together. In the vision of renewal that belongs to Catholic Quakerism the clergyman has no place at all. One of the objectives of George Fox's movement for Christian renewal was the removal of the clergy from the life of the church. Fox envisaged renewal as a movement in which the clergy would play no part.

The Rebirth of the Laity

The third type of renewal—the rebirth of the laity—is a movement that is taking place in the context of certain assumptions that underlie everything that is being done. The first of these assumptions is that the church must have its institutional side as well as its spiritual side, and "there must be no playing of charisma and institution against one another." Second is the assumption that, whatever changes occur in the role of either clergy or laity, they do not denigrate the clergy, and finally, it is assumed that renewal is something that will take place within the inherited structure of Christianity, and that it will not seriously tamper with the essential features of this structure but leave them intact. Howard Grimes says, "The traditional Protestant descriptions of the Church list only two 'marks': preaching and the administration of the sacraments," and in all that he says about *The Rebirth of the Laity* he assumes that corporate worship, and preaching, and the celebration of the sacraments will be continued. "I am concerned" he says, "with patterns and structures which will supplement the traditional work of the church."[34]

Pietism

I wish to maintain that renewal that goes forward on the basis of these assumptions is a certain kind of renewal, and the name of this kind of renewal is Pietism. I also want to point out that Fox's vision of renewal made none of these assumptions, and consequently his strategy of renewal has a very different shape and character from the patterns of renewal that have here been under review.

As far as I know, Pietism is the only strategy of renewal that has been produced by the Protestant ethos in the Protestant era. In the Protestant world, renewal and Pietistic procedures have been so closely identified that to speak of the Pietistic approach to renewal sometimes seems a little absurd to the Protestant mind.

Because Pietism has furnished the classical strategy for Christian renewal in the Protestant Era, it is now calling the tune of renewal in the Ecumenical Movement. Because the acceptance of Pietism implies the death sentence for the vision of renewal that belongs to Catholic Quakerism, we are compelled to make it an object of critical study.

Catholic Quakerism stands in a different relation to Pietism than do the different traditions within Protestantism because it is the bearer of a vision of renewal that is a rival alternative to the

Pietistic conception of renewal. Catholic Quakerism does not accept the presuppositions on which Pietism is based, and it is committed to challenge these presuppositions. Pietism, and its presuppositions, are everywhere present on the Protestant scene and in the Ecumenical Movement. It is not often identified by name, and it is not often the subject of critical study. It has become the standard Protestant approach to renewal because it is an approach that is congenial to the spirit of Protestantism.

Anabaptism and Quakerism both had their beginnings before the rise of Pietism in the 18th century. Pietism has had its impact on both Anabaptist and Quaker church life and, in so far as both these traditions became protestantized in the 19th and 20th centuries, it has been chiefly the work of a Pietist leadership and by means of Pietist techniques. Because of these circumstances it is of special importance for those who stand within the Anabaptist and Quaker traditions to look at Pietism in a different way from those who stand within the various Protestant traditions.

It is therefore a necessary part of this study to describe briefly the anatomy of Pietism in terms of five basic characteristics. We have already noted its acceptance of institutional Christianity with word, sacrament, and ordained ministry as an acceptable framework for its activities.

A chief feature of Pietism is its individualistic conception of salvation. For the Pietist the salvation that the gospel brings is personal salvation. What is known as "Revivalism" is the method of gospel preaching that was inspired by Pietism. The object of revivalistic preaching is to evoke a personal response. The evangelist does not need to represent any particular church fellowship, and his appeal need not include a call to become gathered into any particular church fellowship. The revivalist emphasizes personal faith and makes fellowship subordinate to faith. Fellowship is something that is added to faith as a secondary thing. The church is subsidiary to faith. It is a mere external aid to faith. Some of the best known revivalistic preachers have left the choice of church fellowship entirely to the new convert, and this plainly implies that it doesn't matter much which of the existing denominations he chooses. In the few cases where new denominations have been formed as a result of Pietistic preaching and activity, it has not been by deliberate intent.

The Pietistic conception of Christian Ethics is also individualistic. Pietist ethics lays the emphasis on individual morality, and it sometimes leads to a high degree of personal morality while, at the same time, remaining blind to the forces of immorality that are destroying society. The Pietist has made no great contribution to the Christian witness against war, or the evils arising from the industrialization of the economic order.

In the matter of eschatology, Pietism tends to be apocalyptic. For the Pietist, nothing is more important than the assurance of his own personal salvation, and he does not see his own salvation as a part of a master plan by which God is redeeming society and history. If God wants to save the world he will do so by some cataclysmic event that will take place in the last times. But there is no clear and direct relationship between the individual's personal salvation and God's plan to save the world.

The Valiant Spirit

From this brief description it should begin to be apparent that Pietism faces the evil world and the institutional church with a spirit which is vastly different from the valiant spirit that belongs to the vision of Catholic Quakerism. Catholic Quakerism is at war with the evil in the hearts of men and in the institutions of society, and it is at war with the false church. This is not a war of man's making. It is the Lamb's war. It has no weapons but spiritual weapons—the power of Christ's Spirit, Christ's Gospel, Christ's Cross.

When Pietism enters its bloodstream, Catholic Quakerism is already on the road to extinction. Pietism brings with it a conception of renewal, a conception of salvation, and a conception of God's work in society and history which eviscerates everything that gives strength of purpose and clarity of vision to the cause of Catholic Quakerism.

Eberhard Arnold, the founder of the Bruderhof, said in 1929 in a letter to the Mennonite, Robert Friedmann, "The prophetic man knows that the Pietist can only create an illusion of peace, because he fails to comprehend the objectivity of the kingdom of God. Prophetism is far removed from Pietism. All that they have in common is the sense of being personally spoken to by God himself, the personal experience that God is and that he is interested in man. The tremendous chasm between the two consists in the fact that the Pietist feels satisfied when he experiences the personal sense of salvation and the presence of the personal God, whereas the prophetic spirit thereby only comes to the sense of committing himself to the decisive work of God and thereby desires, without any consideration for his personal feeling of happiness, to see the will of God realized for the whole world."[35]

The Role of the Quakers

Therefore, to conclude and summarize: If "Solus Christus" is to carry with it certain hidden presuppositions, it cannot be a basis for conversations that Quakers can accept without critical examination. It should be the role of the Quakers in these ecumenical discussions to challenge these presuppositions.

Pietistic presuppositions underlie the movement towards renewal that is now appearing in the several forms mentioned. The vision of renewal that belongs to Catholic Quakerism does not start with these presuppositions, but rather starts by challenging them. Because Catholic Quakerism has its own distinctive approach to renewal it can never take the Pietist approach at its face value.

Chapter V

The Recovery of the Quaker Vision

The Quaker pioneers believed that they had been called to proclaim the beginning of a new era in Christian history. In 1674 Robert Barclay wrote: "And this is that we are persuaded, the Lord is bringing about in our day, though many do not and many will not see it, ... who are now despising Christ in his inward appearance, because of the meanness of it; as the Jews of old did him in his outward: yet notwithstanding there were some then that did witness ... that he was come; even so now there are thousands, that can set to their seal, that he ... is appearing in ten thousands of his saints; in and among whom (as the first fruit of many more that shall be gathered) he is restoring the golden age, and bringing them into the holy order and government of his own Son, who is ruling and to rule in the midst of them, setting forth the counsellors as at the beginning, and judges as at first; and establishing truth, mercy, righteousness and judgment again in the earth..."[1]

The early Quaker story is inspiring, and yet what they did to translate the Quaker vision into reality is not repeatable. Isaac Penington says that, "the angel that [God] sends with the everlasting gospel ... he sends not without his authority; yea, the message that he thus sends in any age hath a particular reference to the state of the world and the state of God's people in that age."[2] The vision is good and true for all men in all ages, but the expression of this vision takes different forms in different ages because the state of the world and the state of the church are continually changing. My plea for the recovery of the Quaker vision is not a plea for the recovery of the 17th century expression of it.

In the second and third chapters I tried to set forth what I believe to be the two principal features of the Quaker vision:

namely, God's call for righteousness and God's call for a holy people to live under his rule. In the Quaker vision, the gospel is understood to be the good news that by the power of Christ this twofold call of God can now be answered in all the fullness that God requires of us. The Quaker vision is centered on Jesus Christ who leads his people into righteousness and leads them into unity and community. This bypasses the greater part of what we commonly associate with "the Christian religion," and it lays the emphasis on God's moral teaching through Christ, and on God's gift of unity and community through Christ. Unity and righteousness have a close relationship to each other in the new covenant because unity is experienced through corporate obedience to the moral truth that Christ teaches his people.

The word "recovery" may seem to imply a digging into the past, and exhuming the bygone dreams and visions of another age. It is true that my own spiritual quest has involved a lot of digging into the past, but I cannot emphasize too strongly that this was not motivated by an antiquarian or archeological interest. My quest was centered on the question, "What was the spiritual dynamic that gave the early Quaker community its power and drive?" I maintain that there was such a dynamic, which I am calling "the Quaker vision," and I believe in the possibility of its recovery.

The Quaker Vision in the World Today

In this concluding chapter I want to discuss the important question: "What is the relation of the Quaker vision to the present-day Quaker community?" But first I want to consider a question of even greater importance: "What is the relation of the Quaker vision to the state of the world and the state of God's people in this present age?"

It would be absurd to claim that I have the knowledge or capacity to summarize the "state of the world" in a few paragraphs. But for the purpose of this study I will try to say something about the spiritual condition of man in the modern age. H. G. Wood[*] once observed that the man of the middle ages was preoccupied with the ever-present fact of death. He turned to

---

[*]H.G Wood, 1879-1963, preceded Maurice Creasey as Director of Studies at Woodbrooke Quaker College

Christianity for the assurance that there is something beyond the grave. In the age of Reformation men were preoccupied with sin and its consequences. Christianity was seen as the means by which a merciful God had rescued man from the consequences of his sin. The 20th century man is not preoccupied with problems of death and hell but with the problem of his "lostness."

The image of modern man that emerges from modern literature is that of a being whose inner state is best described by the term "alienation." What does "alienation" mean? It means: not knowing where one belongs; not knowing where home is; not having any fixed star to steer by. Fox said, "I warn and charge you all in the presence of the living God that none make this their habitation in the earth ... lest ye become vagabonds from the Lord. But let everyone rest in his habitation in God, and here is no vagabond; but there shall everyone know ... a habitation, and an inheritance."[3] He says that those who forsake the right way, which is Christ, become as "wandering stars"[4] "wandering in strange paths in the dark world,"[5] but "Man's stability is Christ the light, the life, the foundation of God that stands sure."[6] Having found this light we see how we became lost and also see "our way home again."[7] "Follow Jesus Christ," says Fox, "for they that do so are the fixed stars in the firmament of God's power."[8] In William Penn's account of Fox's experience on Pendle Hill he says that Fox had a vision of "people as thick as motes in the sun, that should in time be brought home to the Lord."[9]

For many people in our time there are no fixed stars to steer by, and no idea where home is. We often hear it said that this is an age of moral relativism. In ethical matters men have lost sight of the pole star and cannot tell where true North is. Everyman does what is right in his own eyes, and moral confusion prevails.

It is also a common complaint in our time that men have lost the secret of living together. There is a great longing for community and yet, in the midst of crowds, men are lonely. Age-old patterns of home and family life have broken down. Modern man is involved in the life of many organizations and institutions which leave his yearning for community unfulfilled.

The Recovery of the Quaker Vision

The man of today does not understand history in terms of God's self-revelation in historical events. He sees history as a social process, and he knows that he is involved in this process, and that his life is largely determined by it. "He does not feel himself to be an actor in a great and dramatic destiny..."[10] For him the forces of history are impersonal rather than personal, moral, and spiritual forces.

The great social force of our time is that combination of financial, technological, and military forces that we call modern civilization. Modern man, says Walter Lippmann, is "subject to the massive powers of our civilization, forced to adopt their pace, bound to their routine, entangled in their conflicts." These forces bear down upon him with a ruthless compulsion as great as that of any king or priest. Life in our modern industrial civilization becomes depersonalized and dehumanized. A new type of man has appeared who exists to facilitate the processes of mass production and mass consumption, and in whom the power of free choice has become atrophied. He is not bound by tyrannical leaders, laws, or institutions. He is free to think and decide what he likes. But because his interior life is without moral, social, or historical absolutes, the privilege of free choice is an empty one. We call this new type of man the mass man. He is not an illiterate peasant or a mere clod. He is constantly bombarded by such mass media as newspapers, periodicals, radio, television, movies. He is skillful, successful, prosperous, but his life is not held together by any single thread of meaning. Unscrupulous political leaders, by controlling the mass media, can control the mass man.

The "Outsider"

How long can men live in a moral vacuum? How long can they hunger for true community in the midst of a multitude of organizational commitments? How long can men be content to let life happen to them without agonizing over its meaning? Apparently millions of people can put up with this state of affairs for a very long time. But the human spirit eventually rebels against a comfortable, secure, but meaningless existence. Man was not created to live in a state of peace without understanding.

Chapter V

And so there is emerging, over against the terrors and comforts of mass existence, another type of man who is in open rebellion against the patterns of life imposed by modern industrial civilization. One of the names that has been given to this type of man is the "Outsider." The "Outsider" has been defined as one who is seeking for a religious solution to the problem of the meaning of existence without the help of the revealed religion of the Hebrew and Christian traditions. This means that he accepts, as part of the "given-ness of life," that there are no moral, social, or historical absolutes in it. Meaning, for the "Outsider", must be found in spite of the absence of these absolutes. This certainly narrows the field in which meaning can be found. The "Outsider" has been forced to seek meaning in terms of the fact of his own existence, and of the range of choices open to him in human existence, and particularly in his own existence. He finds a way of escape from the rigid patterns of civilized life by asserting his power of volition, and by deliberately choosing a pattern of life for himself that expresses his defiance of those social forces that are pressing men into a common mold. The "Outsider" is therefore usually described as an existentialist, and sometimes describes himself by that term.

The most conspicuous feature in the life of the "Outsider" is a feature of which he does not seem always to be consciously aware. This is his flat rejection of the testimony of the Hebrew and Christian scriptures. He is dimly aware that his forefathers had a vital religion that gave them the assurance that there was an order in the universe which justified their lives because they were a part of it. Yet he feels that he must take, as his starting point, the renunciation of the heritage of prophetic religion. He is one who is seeking for a religious solution to the problem of alienation without the help of God's revelation in history.

Perhaps the prototype for all modern "Outsiders" was Nietzsche. It was he who first made the proclamation: "God is dead." This is not a statement from the viewpoint of the atheist. It is not a statement that there never was a God, or that there is no need for the hypothesis of a god. It is rather the proclamation that the God whose self-revelations furnished man with the foundations for an objective morality, the belief in the possibility of a

The Recovery of the Quaker Vision

God-ruled community, and the sense that there is meaning and purpose in history—this God, the God of Abraham, Isaac and Jacob and the Father of our Lord and Savior Jesus Christ—is no longer the living God of Western man. Men no longer meet the God of the prophets and apostles in living encounter. This God has become as lifeless as Woden and Thor.

The theme "God is dead" has become one of the principal themes of modern literature. If the problem of alienation has become the central human problem of the 20th century, is it not because the living God of truth has ceased to be a reality for modern man? For the "Outsider", the 23rd Psalm is the description of a divine-human relationship that has ceased to be a human possibility. No shepherd-God leads him into paths of righteousness; the fear of evil remains, but there is no offer of divine help to overcome it, no good and merciful God gives him the assurance that he will dwell in the Lord's house forever. He has become a vagabond, "wandering in strange paths in a dark world."

It is little wonder that he who first proclaimed the death of God was among the first to experience the consequent terrors of alienation. "Where is my home?" cried Nietzsche: "For it do I ask and seek, and have sought, but have not found it. O eternal everywhere, O eternal nowhere, O eternal in vain."

The quest for home will be eternally in vain for the "Outsider" because the whole reason for his alienation stems from the fact that he has rejected the one path that leads home. The answer to the problem of the "Outsider" can only be found on the path of the prophetic faith that produced the Hebrew-Christian scriptures. G. Ernest Wright describes the Bible as "primarily a confessional history in which the acts of God are interpreted as bringing into being a new society which is the divine answer to the alienation and degradation of the people of the world."

But if and when the alienated people of the world begin to find their way home again, will this mean that they will begin to drift back into the institutional churches? Is that little church on the corner, or around the corner, the true spiritual home from which the alienated of the earth have wandered? If this type of

Chapter V

seeker returns to the institutional church, will he find there the moral, social, and historical orientation for which his soul yearns? Will he not find instead moral relativism, group dynamics, and an institution organized for religious purposes? In order to come to the knowledge of the righteousness of God, and to become gathered into a fellowship based on obedience to God's righteousness, must the seeker of today feel compelled to accept the institutional churches as offering the only means of finding these things?

I believe that today, no less than in 1652, there are "people as thick as motes in the sun ... that will in time be brought home to the Lord," but I do not think that this means that they will all become good church members in respectable denominations that have received the seal of approval from the National Council of Churches.* People who have visited the depths of the abyss, and who have experienced the terror of life as it really is apart from God, will scarcely be touched by the stately routines of the ancient institutional churches. Such people will be satisfied with nothing less than a fellowship that hears and obeys the call of Christ to righteousness, and whose life as a fellowship is grounded in the corporate experience of corporate obedience and corporate suffering for the sake of obedience. God calls for righteousness and community, and there is no home for today's spiritual vagabonds short of answering this call.

Some day the "Outsiders" of this present age will discover the man who perhaps ought to be the patron saint of "Outsiders". His name is George Fox. Fox knew the inner state of today's "Outsider" and knew what it was to endure this state of hopeless drifting. Without being addicted to any particular vice, or without being conscious of overt sin, he was nonetheless burdened with a sense of alienation from God, from truth, and from his fellows. He was like a man who had fallen into a very deep sand pit. Every time he tried to climb out, the sand gave way under his feet. There were years on end when he felt himself hopelessly trapped. He says of these years, "When I was in the deep, under all shut up, I could not believe that I should ever

---

* This has been replaced by similar organisations in modern times.

overcome."[11] To the "outsider" of his own day Fox says, "Ye that have been in the wilderness, can witness ... with me, and the same temptations, even to despair, and to make themselves away."[12] Francis Howgill says of his own experience as an "outsider", "I sought death in that day and could not find it."[13] Emil Brunner has written that, "What oxygen is to the lungs and the blood, hope is for the soul."[14] In the extremities of hopeless despair Fox and Howgill sought the help of representatives of institutional religion but could not find help there. But they did nevertheless find a way out of this seemingly escape-proof pit. And when the "outsiders" of today discover this, may this not mark the beginning of a recovery of the Quaker vision?

Modern Quaker Life

Now we must turn to the question which cries for an answer in any discussion of the recovery of the Quaker vision. What are we to say to those who ask: If the Quaker vision is to be recovered, does this imply a special responsibility on the part of those who are the heirs of this vision—the spiritual descendants of the early Quakers who are known today as the Religious Society of Friends? This is the question that has been uppermost in my mind for about twenty-five years. In fact, membership in the Society of Friends seems to me to imply interest in this question. It has been my purpose in these essays to maintain that *the Quaker vision is a universal or catholic vision*, and that it is not only relevant to the inner life of the Quaker denomination, but it is relevant to the state of the world. It is the answer to the predicament of modern man. Can Quakers rightly interpret the signs of the times and also recover the Quaker vision in such a way that there will be a new application of changeless truth in a changing world? There are two factors in modern Quaker life that need to be taken into account as we approach this question.

The first of these factors is the sect-mindedness that seems to have penetrated every pore of Quaker life. In the spectrum of sectarian Christianity, the Quakers of today regard themselves as a Christian society hardly less sectarian in spirit than the Plumstead Peculiars. Not many Friends today would agree with the early Friends that Quakerism is good and true for all men everywhere in all ages, and that it is destined to be the prevailing pattern for the Christianity of the future.

In his 1950 lecture, *Friends at Mid Century*, Elbert Russell said, "Through the years we have been slowed up by love of respectability, awe of majorities, and complacent acceptance of the role of a small sect in a big world."[15] There are some realists who maintain that, whatever Quakerism was intended to be in the beginning, it has now become a sect in fact and we may as well accept the name. There is some logic in this position, but if the Quakers have become a sect by a process of degeneration then the task of renewal must surely mean combating those forces that have caused us to become a sect, and especially the ubiquitous sect-mindedness that blinds us to the need for renewal and robs us of a sense of destiny.

Four Centers of Quakerism

Another feature of Quaker life that will affect the recovery of the Quaker vision is the widely held theory that the Society of Friends is a community with four centers, four traditions, and four styles of language. Since 1952 there has been a generally accepted terminology for these four types of Quakerism, namely: prophetic, mystical, humanitarian, and evangelical.

The stream of Quaker history has not flowed in a single channel but has divided into four different channels. Each channel has its own traditions, its own set of presuppositions, its own frame of reference. World Quakerism today has not one center but four centers, and the Quakers are being defined as a community in which these four centers, and the four streams of experience flowing from them, all exist side by side in a balanced relationship. This state of things has been called "a wise religious pluralism." Keeping the balance between these four elements is considered to be absolutely necessary to the spiritual health of our Society, and Quaker leadership is largely united in the belief that its first concern should be the maintenance of this balance.

Since each of these four traditions has its own style of language, there has arisen a serious crisis of communication in

Quaker life. At a recent Friends General Conference a Friend asked, "Do the conditions for communication exist in the Society of Friends today?" In our Quaker conferences and discussions in recent years there is the outward appearance of a process of communication. But this is largely illusory because each different group of participants lives in its own universe of discourse. Very little that is said is heard by others in the frame of reference in which it is intended to be understood. Modern Quaker discussion moves in a circular motion and returns to its starting point.

One would suppose that all Friends would desire to find a common language so that they could communicate with one another and so become, in truth, a society of Friends. But the fact is that for many Friends the finding of that "perfect oneness" for which Fox pleaded would destroy everything that they value most in Quakerism. They consider our present confusion of tongues a small price to pay for the individual freedom that this present Quaker chaos makes possible. The spiritual and intellectual atmosphere that I have been describing is not conducive to real dialogue. Discussion becomes an end in itself, and it tends to degenerate into a formal routine which is not a dynamic process leading to consensus.

I have often heard the comment that Quakerism would be dull and colorless if, instead of four centers, we had only one. I find the notion that the best interests of the Society are served by preventing each of its four traditions from exerting an influence beyond its allotted twenty-five per cent to be a static conception, and one that is spiritually and intellectually suffocating. Another notion that has recently been revived is that Quakerism, by its very nature, involves permanent tension between irreconcilable positions.

As these notions win wider and wider acceptance they come to have the binding power of dogmatic principles. But I refuse to accept these notions. I reject the idea that there is a built-in confusion and a built-in pluralism which are proper to the essential given-ness of Quakerism, and that no one can do anything about it. Friends should be striving to come out of their confusion and pluralism and should, instead, be seeking to recover the "one

Chapter V

steadying central conception" that, according to John Wilhelm Rowntree*, lies at the heart of Quakerism.

The exponents of the four-center theory of Quakerism claim that from the earliest beginnings of historical Quakerism these four elements have been present. And they are right. But this is not to say that from the beginning these four traditions had equal weight, or that they were expected to flow eternally in four separate channels of historical development.

In its beginnings Quakerism was a prophetic faith, and if it contained prophetic, evangelical, mystical, and humanitarian elements, this is because these are all present in prophetic Quakerism. Prophetic Quakerism contains a distinctive type of evangelism. The humanitarianism of early Quakerism is not distinct from its prophetism but is a natural outgrowth of it. There is an emphasis on the inward and spiritual in prophetic Quakerism that is not imported from any of the distinctively mystical traditions. When we place the prophetic element at the center of Quakerism we are not stripping it of its humanitarian, "mystical", and evangelical content. It only means that these elements in Quakerism will cease to go on developing in separate channels, thus creating several different kinds of Quakerism, and furnishing different centers for a plurality of sub-communities within the Society of Friends.

There are some Quakers who feel that the present confusion and pluralism must be endured because there is no feasible alternative. The only alternative that they see is an artificial creedal unity imposed from above. Since all agree that the Society of Friends is not an authoritarian church, there can be no satisfactory remedy by means of church authority.

Confusion or a creed? Is there a third possibility? I believe there is. Fox once suggested that there ought to be a permanent discussion taking place at all times between all the denominations in Christendom He believed in the convincing power of truth, and he maintained that if truth could get a fair hearing

---

* John Wilhelm Rowntree (1868-1905) was a prominent figure in the "Liberal" revival of London (Britain) Yearly Meeting at the close of the 19th century. But note that the word "liberal" now has a rather different meaning in a Quaker context.

the witness of God in men's hearts would cause them to receive it. So what we need is a different kind of discussion than the kind we have been having in recent years. We need more of the kind of discussion in which every participant believes that God is seeking to reveal the right way for all.

As long as Quaker life and thought are hamstrung by the dogma that by its very nature and constitution Quakerism must have four centers, there will be little prospect for the recovery of the Quaker vision by Quakers.

The Implications of the Quaker Vision

Whether the Quaker vision is recovered by Quakers or by others, its recovery will have far-reaching implications. I want now to examine some of these implications. I have already made some observations about the spiritual state of man in the modern world, and I want to conclude with some observations about the present and future state of the church.

The institutional church of today, in both its Protestant and Roman Catholic forms, is going through a process of self-criticism and reformation on a scale that surpasses anything the world has seen since the death of Cromwell. In the Protestant world this new reforming spirit has three major objectives: first, to re-gather the scattered fragments of denominational Christianity into a visible unity; second, to release Christianity from captivity to Western culture; and, third, to direct the gaze of the church toward the need of the world rather than toward its own inner well-being as a religious organization.

The institutional church has become aware that in its traditional forms it cannot adequately relate itself to the state of the world in the 20th century. The churches are stressing that their drive to find reunification and renewal is for the sake of fulfilling their role in the modern world. And what is this role if it is not to combat the evils in our secularized society by a superior religious force, emanating from a revitalized institutional church? When the institutional church looks into the future, it sees a church that has been radically transformed. But it is still an institutional church and, moreover, it is continuous with the institutional church through the ages.

Chapter V

But this dream of the institutional church is not the only way to envisage the church of the future. Oliver Quick once said that it may be that the church of the future will seek to "be rid of the burdens and responsibilities of a so-called Christian civilization and start its career all over again as a colony of heaven in a Christ-denying world."[16] It should be the task of the Quakers to make this second possibility a live option in the 20th century.

James Hastings Nichols concludes his History of Christianity 1650-1950 by putting before us two visions for the church of the future in these words:

> The modern Christian churches inherited the great new enterprise of mediaeval and Reformation Christianity, the endeavor to penetrate and "Christianize" civilization. For three hundred years they have continued this attempt, yet, on the whole, with ever less success. There are, one might guess, as great a proportion of convinced and practicing Christians as ever. But the great forces and structures of modern civilization have increasingly eluded Christian guidance and have promised new gods, tribal and Utopian. In recent years Christians have become increasingly aware of the width of the chasm between the tone of the industrial west and anything that might be called Christian. It does not yet appear how they will adjust to this situation. Will they return to the policy of the church in the ancient Roman Empire, in which, whether persecuted or recognized by the state, the church entertained no serious hope of transforming state and society, but sought rather to manifest another quality of life within its own community? Or will the church continue to seek, and perhaps find, some way of humanizing and rendering responsive to Jesus Christ a militarized, technological, mass civilization?

The choice that Nichols puts before us is a false choice, because it fails to understand that the church which manifests a quality or style of life through corporate obedience and suffering is releasing a transforming power into society. The power by which God chooses to redeem society and history is the power of the cross. The attempt of the ancient ecclesiastical institutions to penetrate and "Christianize" civilization has failed, and any renewed attempts of this kind will also fail. But the alternative is not, as Nichols maintains, to lose hope in the possibility of world redemption and choose instead to cultivate the inner life of a church which has withdrawn from society and history. The true church of the cross may be rejected by the world, but it is not withdrawn from the world. The Anabaptists and Quakers are frequently cited by Protestant church historians as classic examples of the "church withdrawn." Yet these groups were the pioneers of all modern missionary activity and carried the whole burden of the church's missionary task when the Protestant world was still blind to it.

Both Anabaptists and Quakers have become "churches withdrawn" in certain phases of their history, but this is not a part of the Quaker vision. For Fox, the suffering community of the Suffering Servant is God's way of saving God's world. The servant church is not above its Lord. The alternative that the Quaker vision opposes to institutional Christianity is not the "church withdrawn," but a church which has discovered the true nature and source of world-redeeming power. It should be the task of the heirs of the Quaker vision to witness for the church of the cross and to make this genuine alternative to institutional Christianity a live option in this present age.

The Disciple Church Community

In conclusion, I want to say two things about the disciple church of the future. First, I want to draw attention to the primary character of the disciple church community and, second, I want to say a word about the distinctive character of the evangelism of the future that belongs to this vision of the church of the future.

Now, what is meant by the statement: "the disciple church is a primary community"? A primary community is one that has the first claim on our loyalty and is the social force that has the greatest influence on our lives. It is our basic social orientation and the group which, more than any other, we feel to be the place where we belong. It is the social commitment that determines all other social commitments. It is a fact that for many

Chapter V

people today church membership does not mean membership in a primary community. James Pike says, "Companies, unions, political parties, clubs and clinics ... become more important than the religious and ethical outlook in shaping the lives of church members."*

For early Friends, the Quaker community was the primary community, and following their loyalty to the meeting came all the other loyalties in a descending scale, i.e., loyalty to family, civil government, and business. For many Friends today this scale of loyalties has become reversed, with the business commitment playing the primary role in shaping and determining the pattern of life, and with the Christian social orientation coming in a poor fourth. Membership in the disciple church of the future must mean a primary commitment that determines and regulates all other social commitments.

I believe that this community will reappear in history by the same means by which it has always been brought into existence, namely, by the work of evangelism. The term "evangelism" has been devaluated for many people today because it has been tied to an individualistic conception of salvation and has consequently seen its task to consist in evoking from the individual a personal decision that has consequences for his own soul's welfare. But the gospel is not only good news for the individual; it is good news for the world. God, who created the world and saw that it was good, also loved the world and sent Jesus to redeem it. The good news must also proclaim that Christ has come to be the head and governor of God's people, and that he leads this newly created people into righteousness. He teaches them the principles of God's righteousness and draws them into a unity of witness for the truth of these principles. God has called this community into existence to be the instrument of his purpose of world redemption. The meaning of history is bound up with the history of this community.

If the gospel is to deliver modern men from their sense of alienation, it must be proclaimed with all the fullness of its moral, social, and historical implications. This does not mean

*We cannot source this reference.

that the gospel is a religious theory to be accepted or rejected. It involves personal decision—the Lord of history and the Master of the disciple church must become my Lord and Master too. But the meaning and content of the evangel needs to be expanded and set free from the limitations of a narrow religious individualism.

The gospel, says Brunner, should be "a word from the fellowship of faith leading to the fellowship of faith."[17] "The word of witness is not the Word of an individual, but a Word spoken from fellowship, the Word which because it bears witness to Jesus Christ at the same time bears witness to a fellowship, to the brotherhood of the Ekklesia, which has its origin in Him ... Where the witness is true and vital it creates Ekklesia, the brotherhood that tears down all barriers which otherwise divide the historical and earthly world of men: the barriers of race, of class, of nationality, of sex."[18]

For the Quaker vision, which is the vision of the disciple church, this is the winter season. But I believe the end of this winter may be already in sight. This is a time to remember the words of Fox to those who refused the Quaker vision in the 17th century: "Do you think you can keep it always winter or stop the summer from coming?"[19]

Appendix

George Fox wrote or dictated two summaries of the three-hour sermon he gave on Firbank Fell in 1652, which resulted in the conversion of large numbers of people, including some who became outstanding missioners and leaders of the early Quaker movement. The first of these is contained in the autobiographical account dictated to Thomas Lower in 1675 and now known as the *Spence manuscript*. It was included in somewhat altered form in Thomas Ellwood's edition of the *Journal*, published in 1694. I have chosen to reprint it from the *Journal* as edited by John L. Nickalls (Cambridge University Press, 1952 and 1975), p. 109, which restores the original text of the Spence ms:

> I was made to open to the people that the steeplehouse and that ground on which it stood were no more holy than that mountain, and those temples and "dreadful houses of God", (as they called them) were not set up by the command of God nor Christ; nor their priests as Aaron's priesthood; nor their tithes as theirs was. But Christ was come, who ended the temple, and the priests, and the tithes, and Christ said, "Learn of me", and God said, "This is my beloved Son, hear ye him." For the Lord had sent me with his everlasting gospel to preach, and his word of life to bring them off all those temples, tithes, priests and rudiments of the world, that had gotten up since the apostles' days, and had been set up by such who had erred from the spirit and power the apostles were in; so that they might all come to know Christ their teacher, their counsellor, their shepherd to feed them, and their bishop to oversee them and their prophet to open to them, and to know their bodies to be the temples of God and Christ for them to dwell in.
>
> And so I opened the prophets and the figures and shadows and turned them to Christ the substance, and then

Appendix

opened the parables of Christ and the things that had been hid from the beginning, and showed them the estate of the Epistles how they were written to the elect; and the state of the apostacy that has been since the apostles' days, and how the priests have got the Scriptures and are not in that spirit which gave them forth; who make a trade of their words and have put them into chapter and verse; and how that the teachers and priests now are found in the steps both of the false prophets, chief priests, scribes, and Pharisees, such as both the prophets, Christ, and his apostles cried against, and so are judged by the prophets', Christ's and the apostles' spirit; and all that were in it could not own them. And so turning the people to the spirit of God, and from the darkness to the light that they might believe in it and become children of the light, and turning them from the power of Satan which they had been under to God, and that with the spirit of Truth they might be led into all the Truth of the prophets', Christ's and the apostles' words.

Fox's second summary of his sermon on Firbank Fell was prepared in 1689 for inclusion in *The Memory of the Righteous Revived*, a collection of the writings of two of the outstanding converts on that occasion. It was published in the same year, thus appearing in print five years before his 1675 account. It is here reprinted from *Narrative Papers of George Fox*, edited by Henry J. Cadbury (Richmond, Ind.: Friends United Press, 1972), pp. 167-168:

> The Testimony of George Fox, Concerning our Dear Friends and Brethren John Audland, and John Camm ...
>
> When George Fox came to Furbanck Chapel in Westmorland, John Audland and Francis Howgill was preaching there in the morning, but they Preacht freely; and there came Major Bousfield and Col. Benson, and they were free Preachers in Yorkshire also; And in the Afternoon there was a great gathering of People more than in the Morning, and so the House would not hold them, and so I was moved to go upon a Mountain hard by, and the People gathered to the Mountain, and sat down; though it was then a strange thing to have Meetings anywhere but in the

Appendix

Church, so called, because it was holy Ground, they thought. People were so ignorant then: So after sometime I stood up, and said unto them, That that Ground was as holy as any other, and that Christ did meet upon a Mountain, and by the Sea side, and in Houses, and so did his Apostles and Disciples; and though the Jews had a Temple called holy, in the Old Testament and a Worship there, yet Christ had ended that Temple and Worship and set up a Worship in Spirit and Truth, and all the true Believers in Christ, that received him and his Gospel of Life and Salvation were the true Christians, and their Bodies were the Temples of God, and Christ, & of the holy Ghost; and many other weighty things were opened in that great Assembly, and Many Hundreds were turned from Darkness to Light, and from the Power of Satan to God, and received the Grace and Truth that comes by Jesus, and by it received Christ in their Hearts; and many other precious Truths were opened to them that Day: And though the Apostles went into the Jews' Synagogues and Temple, it was not to hold them up, but to bring People off the Jews' Ways, Traditions and Ceremonies, to Christ the Substance, for he was come, and is come, the same Today, as he was Yesterday, and so forever, a Leader, a Governour, a Prophet, a Bishop, a Shepherd, and a Priest, to exercise his Heavenly Offices in his People, his living Members, his Church which he is the holy Head of, and a King to Rule in their Hearts by Faith; and as I said before, many hundreds received God's Truth that Day; and Immediately after that Christ the Son of God was revealed in them, John Audland and John Camm, and several others, went forth and Preacht Christ, and his Everlasting Gospel;

Kingston upon Thames, the 7th of the 4th Month, 1689.

George Fox.

Appendix

FOR FURTHER READING about the message of George Fox, see the following publications, available from various Quaker outlets;

Lewis Benson, *What did George Fox teach about Christ?* New Foundation Publications no. 1, 1976.
Lewis Benson, *The Quaker Vision*, New Foundation Publications no. 4, 1979.
Lewis Benson, *The Truth Is Christ*, New Foundation Publications no. 55, 1981.
Joseph Pickvance, *Christ in Quaker Thought and Practise*, New Foundation Publications no.6, 1993.
Annette Fricke, *George Fox Speaks to Me*, New Foundation Publications no.7, 1997.
Terry Smith Wallace, editor, *None were so clear: Prophetic Quaker Faith and the Ministry of Lewis Benson*, New Foundation Publications, US, 1995
Kennard T. Wing, *Champion of a Forgotten Faith: the Life and Ministry of Lewis Benson*, New Foundation Papers, no.91, 2006.
Douglas Gwyn, *Apocalypse of the Word: The Life and Message of George Fox*, Friends United Press, 1984
Journal of George Fox, rev.ed.John L. Nickalls, reprint Philadelphia, 1997
Joseph Pickvance, *A Reader's Companion to George Fox's Journal*, reprint Curlew Productions, 2001

References

Chapter I
A Fourth Point of View
1. Gardiner, S.R., *History of the Commonwealth and Protectorate* (London: 1897), II, 20-21.
2. Davies, Horton, *The English Free Churches* (London, N.Y., Toronto: Oxford Univ. Press, 1952), p. 198
3. Dillenberger, J., & Welch, C., *Protestant Christianity* (N.Y.: Scribner's Sons, 1954), p. 118
4. Nuttall, G. F., *The Holy Spirit in Puritan Faith and Experience* (Oxford: Blackwell, 1946), p. 13.
5. Ibid., p.14.
6. Ibid., p.14.
7. Horton, Davies, *The English Free Churches*, p. 109.
8. Fox, George, *Works of* (Phila.: Marcus T. Gould; N. Y.: Isaac T. Hopper, 1831), IV, 292.
9. Ibid, III, pp. 372, 461, 552.
10. Ibid, VI, 400; III, 372.
11. Scott, Richenda, *Tradition and Experience* (Swarthmore Lecture, 1964, London: Alien & Unwin), p.10
12. Loukes, Harold, *Friends World News*, Dec. 1954.

Catholic Quakerism
13. Fox, *Works* (1831), III, 5.
14. Penington, Isaac, *Works* (London: Samuel Clark, 1761), I, 59.
15. Barclay, Robert, *Apology* (1678), Prop.X, Section V, p.195.
16. Fox, Manuscripts bound with the Annual Catalogue of Geo. Fox's Papers, p. 85, Catalogue No. 85E.
17. Fox, *Works* (1831), IV, 270.
18. Ibid., VII, 324.
19. Penington, *Works* (1761), I, 223-224.
20. Ibid., 224.
21. Fox, *Journal* (Cambridge, 1911), II, 171.
22. Fox, *Works* (1831), III, 31.
23. Penington, *Works* (1761), II, 500.
24. Fox, *Works* (1831), III, 191.
25. Ibid., III, 99.
26. Fox, *Journal* (Cambridge: Univ. Press, 1952), p.36.
27. Ibid., p.34-35.

The Ground, Root and Foundation
28. Brunner, Emil, *The Divine-Human Encounter* (Phila.: Westminster Press, 1943), p. 127-128.
29. Fox, *Works* (1831), VI, 4.
30. Ibid., III, 458.
31. Brunner, *Revelation and Reason* (Phila.: Westminster Press, 1946), p. 28.

References

The Three Essentials
32. De Dietrich, Suzanne, *The Witnessing Community* (Phila.: Westminster Press, 1958), p. 23.

A Dialogic Relationship to God
33. Fox, *Works* (1831), VII, 281.
34. Fox, *Journal* (London: Headley Bros., Bi-Centenary Edition, 1902), I, 424.
35. Fox, *Works* (1831), IV, 85.
36. Ibid., III, 194
37. Ibid., IV, 69
38. Ibid., IV, 298
39. Isaiah 42:16, quoted by Fox, *Works* (1831), VI, 395
40. Fox, *Works* (1831), VIII, 31
41. Fox, *Journal* (1952), p. 19.
42. Fox, *Journal* (1902), II, 492.

The True and Sure Foundation
43. Fox, *Works* (1831), III, 496.
44. Ibid., IV, 70.
45. Fox, *Journal* (1902), II, 393.
46. Fox, *Works* (1831), VII, 137.
47. Ibid., VIII, 37
48. Ibid., VII, 348
49. Ibid., VIII, 128-129.
50. Ibid., III, 466
51. Penington, *Works* (1761), II, 381-382 p. 45.

Chapter II
Righteousness and Community
1. Fox, *Works* (1831) III, 553.
2. Ibid., III 538
3. Ibid., VII, 258-259
4. Penington, *Works* (1761), I, 556.
5. Penn, William, *Christian Quaker* (W. Penn & Geo. Whitehead, 1673), p. 15
6. *The Christian Answer* (N.Y. Scribner's Sons, 1945, Ed., H.P.Van Dusen) p.165.
7. Ibid., p. 175.

Christ, the Teacher of Righteousness
8. Fox, *Journal* (1952), p. 135
9. Fox, *Works* (1831), III. 68.
10. Ibid., III, 69
11. Ibid., III. 68
12. Ibid., III, 483
13. Ibid., III. 307
14. Ibid., IV. 154
15. Ibid., IV. 32.
16. Epistles and Queries of Geo. Fox, p. 24, Cat. No. 19.47A.
17. Headley Mss., p.154, Cat. No. 7,112F
18. Fox, Works (1831), VII, 33.
19. Ibid., IV. 126 (see Deut. 18:15&18)

The Consequences of a Personal Relationship with Christ
20. Ibid., VII. 313
21. Headley Mss., p. 243, Cat. No. 25,14F.
22. Fox, *Works* (1831), III, 432.
23. Ibid., VII. 323.
24. Ibid., VII. 61

Christian Liberty
25. Brunner, *Man in Revolt* (N.Y.: Scribner's Sons, 1939), pp. 262-263.
26. Penington, *Works* (1761), I, 116
27. Fox, *Works* (1831), IV, 20
28. Ibid., III 69.
29. Ibid., VII. 102
30. Fox, Journal (1902)

Gospel Freedom
31. Ibid., II, 339.
32. Ibid., II. 242.
33. Ibid., 2. II. 338
34. Ibid., II, 339.
35. Fox, *Works* (1831), VII, 88
36. Ibid., VII, 311
37. Ibid., VII, 312
38. Headley Mss. p.315, Cat. No. 8,90F
39. Richardson Mss. Typewritten transcript, p. 215.
40. Ibid., p. 221
41. Fox, *Works* (1831), IV, 361
42. Fox, *Journal* (1902), II. 494

Corporate Obedience
43. Ibid., II, 454
44. Fox, *Works* (1831), VI, 273.
45. Ibid., IV, 271
46. Ibid., VII, 310
47. Ibid., VII, 340.
48. Ibid., VI, 73
49. Fox, *Journal* (1902), I. 15
50. Hopper, Stanley. R. *The Crisis of Faith* (N.Y. Abingdon-Cokebury, 1944) p.307
51. Fox, *Works* (1831) VI. 370.

The Role of the Church
52. *Concern* No.1 (a pamphlet series, Herald Press, Scotidale, PA. June 1954) p.45.
53. Ibid., p.48
54. Ibid., pp.46-47
55. *Concern* No.8. (May 1966) p.27.

Chapter III
The Quaker Conception of Christian Community
1. Richardson Mss., Typewritten transcript, p.125
2. Fox, *Works* (1831), V, 203.

Church Government and Order
3. Ibid., VII, 348; VIII, 129.
4. Fox, *Journal* (1902), II, 442.
5. Ibid., I, 241
6. Fox, *Journal* (1952) p.364
7. Fox, *Works* (1831) VIII.61
8. Ibid., VIII, 206
9. Ibid., VIII, 78
10. Richardson Mss., Typewritten transcript, p. 407.
11. Fox, *Works* (1831), VIII, 184.
12. Ibid., VIII, 37
13. Ibid., VIII, 184
14. Fox, *Journal* (1952), pp. 299, 441.
15. Fox, *Works* (1831), VIII, 137
16. Penington, *Works* (1761), I, 678.
17. Fox, *Works* (1831) V. 450.

The Authority in the Gospel
18. Fox, *Journal* (1902), II, pp. 243, 336. *Works* (1831), VII, 326
19. Fox, *Works* (1831), IV, 102
20. Ibid., VII, 348
21. Fox, *Journal* (1902), II, 240-241
22. Fox, *Works* (1831), VII, 272
23. Cadbury, Henry J. Ed. *Annual Catalogue of George Fox's Papers* (1939) p.64, Cat. No.25C
24. Fox, *Works* (1831), VII, 227, 322
25. Ibid., VII, 227.
26. Ibid., VII, 218.
27. Ibid., VIII, 67.

The Call to Community
28. Jones, R. M., *New Studies in Mystical Religion* (N.Y.: Macmillan, 1928), p. 167.

References

29. Fox. *Works* (1831) VIII. 207
30. Ibid., VIII, 206
31. Fox, *Journal* (1902), II, 436-437.

The Victory of the Lamb
32. Ibid., II, 421.
33. Ibid., II, 176.
34. Fox, *Works* (1831) IV, 177.
35. Ibid., IV, 238.
36. Ibid., VII, 207.
37. Ibid., VI, 426-427
38. Fox, *Journal* (1902), I, 451.

The True Church and False
39. Haller, Wm., *The Rise of Puritanism* (N. Y.: Harper Bros., 1957), p. 173.
40. Penington, *Works* (1761), I, 139.
41. Ibid., I, 122.
42. Ibid., I, 304-305.
43. Ibid., I, clxxxii-clxxxiii
44. Ibid., I, 188.
45. Ibid., I, 211.

But Ye must come out of it all
46. Ibid., I, 30.
47. Headley Mss., p. 303, Cat. No. 8.G9F

Chapter IV
Catholic Quakerism and the Ecumenical Movement
1. *Faith and Order Trends* (Montreal: Sept. 1963), Vol. 3, No. 4, p. 3.
2. A. C. Outler, *The Christian Tradition and the Unity We Seek* (N. Y.Oxford Univ.Press, 1957), p. 17.
3. Ibid., p. 8.
4. *Faith and Order Trends*, Vol. 3, No. 4, p. 3.
5. *The Old and the New in the Church* (World Council of Churches Com. on Faith and Order, Minneapolis: Augsburg Press, 1961), p. 57.
6. Ibid., p. 56.
7. Gustafson, James M., *Treasure in Earthen Vessels* (N. Y. Harper & Bros.1961), p5
8. *The Old and the New in the Church*, p. 78.
9. Brunner, Dogmatics HI (London: Lutterworth Press, 1962), p. 30.
10. Ibid., p. 33.
11. Ibid., p. 30.
12. Ibid., p. 30.
13. Ibid., p. 32.
14. Ibid., p. 129.
15. Kraemer, A *Theology of the Laity* (Phila.: Westminster Press, 1958), pp. 180-181.
16. *Faith and Order Findings*, Final Report, Montreal, 1963 (Minneapolis: Augsburg Press, 1963) Part I, Christ and the Church, Section II, p. 24.
17. The Old and the New in the Church, p. 76.

Tradition and the Traditions
18. *The Christian Tradition and the Unity We Seek*, pp. 128-129
19. Ibid., p. 129.
20. *The Old and the New in the Church*, p. 49
21. *Faith and Order Trends*, Vol. 3, No. 4, p. 5.
22. *The Christian Tradition and the Unity We Seek*, pp. 9, 57.
23. Tomkins, Oliver, *A Time for Unity* (London: SCM Press,

References

1964), p. 78
24. Ibid., p. 114.

Lay Responsibility
25. Grimes, Howard, *The Rebirth of the Laity* (N. Y.: Abingdon Press, 1962), pp. 143-144.
26. Ibid., p. 146.

Lay Vocation
27. Fox, *Works* (1831), IV, 325.
28. Ibid., IV, 337-338
29. Headley Mss., p. 379, Cat. No. 8,100.
30. Fox, *Works* (1831), VI, 41.
31. *A Theology of the Laity*, p. 161.
32. *Evanston Speaks* (London: SCM Press, 1954), p. 104.
33. Congar, Yves M. J., *Lay People in the Church* (1957). Cited by Kraemer, op. cit, p. 11.

Rebirth of the Laity
34. *The Rebirth of the Laity*, pp. III, 112

The Valiant Spirit
35. Friedmann, Robert, *Mennonite Piety Through the Centuries* (Mennonite Historical Society, Goshen, Ind.: 1949), p.88

Chapter V
Recovery of the Quaker Vision
1. Barclay, *The Anarchy of the Ranters*, in *Truth Triumphant* (London, 1692), p. 210.
2. Penington, *Works* (1761), II, 452-453.

The Quaker Vision in the World Today
3. Fox, *Works* (1831), VII, 158.
4. Ibid., VI, 313.
5. Ibid., VII, 218

6. Ibid., III, 510.
7. Headley Mss. p. 303, Cat. No. 8,68F.
8. Fox, *Works* (1831) VI, 259
9. Fox, *Journal* (1952), p. xl.
10. Lippmann, Walter, *A Preface to Morals* (N. Y.: Macmillan Co., 1929), p. 9.

The Outsider
11. Fox, *Journal* (1952) p.12.
12. Fox, *Works* (1831), VII, 55.
13. Howgill, Francis, *Works* (1676) p.43.
14. Brunner, *The Scandal of Christianity* (Phila.: Westminster Press, 1951), p.102.

Modern Quaker Life
15. Russell, Elbert, *Friends at Mid Century* (Johnson Lecture 1950; Five Years Meeting, Richmond, Ind.) p. 32.

The Implications of the Quaker Vision
16. Quick, Oliver, *The Gospel of the New World* (London: Nisbet & Co. 1944), p.107

The Disciple Church Community
17. Brunner, *Dogmatics* III, p.135.
18. Ibid., p.184.
19. Fox, Manuscripts bound with the *Annual Catalogue of Geo. Fox's Papers*, p. 119, Catalogue No.106E.

Index

Abraham, 11, 16
admonition, 31
alienation, 72–77, 84
America, church in, 34, 35
Anabaptism, 35–36, 67
apostasy, 17, 18–19
Arnold, Eberhard, 68–69
authority, 45

Barbour, Hugh, 48
Barclay, Robert, 70
Bible: as standard of righteousness, 23, 26, 27; Quakers view of, 11, 41
Brethren, Church of, 35
Brunner, 15, 28, 55, 77, 85
Burrough, Edward, 10–11

Calvin, John, 5
Calvinism, 22
Catholic Quakerism, *passim*, 10–14
cell group, 62–64
"Chaplains in Industry", 60
charisma, 55, 58
Christ. *See* Jesus Christ
"Christ alone," 59
Christ-centered, 6
Christian Ethics, 20–36
Christian liberty, 28–29
Christian Platonism, 2–3
Christian renewal, 60–61
church: not a religious institution, 38; role of, 33–35
church discipline, Quaker concept of, 31–32
Church Government and Order, 42
church of the cross, 35–36, *See* Disciple Church
church renewal, 81

"church withdrawn", 83
clergy, role of, 60, 61–62
community, 2, 15, 17, 21, 23, 26–28, 37–41, 42–44, 71, 83–85
community, Christian, 32
Congar, Yves M.J., 65
conscience, 23
Constantinian church, 34
corporate obedience, 31–33, 35
corporate suffering, 33
covenant, the old and the new. *See* old covenant; new covenant
cross, meaning of the, 9

David, 11
Davies, Horton, 7, 8
de Dietrich, Suzanne, 15
"death of God", 74
dialogic relationship to God, 14, 15, 16–18, 37, *See* also master–disciple relationship
Dillenberger, J., 7
disciple church, 32–33, 83–85, *See also* church of the cross
discipline, church, 25–28, 30
disownment, not punitive, 30
docetism, ecclesiastical, 56

ecumenical movement, 7, 33, 52–69
ekklesia, 55
eschatology, 68
ethic of idealism, 20–21
ethic of obligation, 21
evangelical Quakerism, 5–6, 8, 78–80, 84–85
Evanston Conference, 62
excommunication, 26, 31
existentialism, 73–76

Index

Faith and Order Findings, 56
Faith and Order Trends, 58
foundation, 14–15, 17, 19, *See also* ground and root
four centers of Quakerism, 78–81
fourth point of view, 6–10
Fox, George: "outsider", 76–77; alternative to professional ministry, 62; Authority of the Church, 42; call to community, 43–44; Christ the Light, 72; christian ethics, 21, 25; christian vocation, 65; church of the cross, 36; clergy, 62; conception of liberty, 26, 28–29; cross of Christ, 42; discipline, 30; evangelical Quakerism, 6; free will, 29; life and the light, 17; light, 23–24; man-made religion, 51; mission of, 13, 42; new covenant, 17, 43; not a religious reformer, 38; order of Christ, 42–43; Pendle Hill, 72; purpose of God, 16; root of Quakerism, 10–11; to Friends in Carolina 1671, 44; Truth, 30; vision of renewal, 65; winter and summer, 85
Frankenstein, 16
free church movement, 35
free will, 29
Friedmann, Robert, 68

Gardiner, S.R., 7
God and man, 14, 15, 16–17, 24, 37
God's righteousness, 22
gospel, 71, 84–85
gospel freedom, 29–30
gospel order, 38–39, 44, 46–47
gospel, sacraments and ministry in institutional church, 53
Grimes, Howard, 63, 66
ground and root of Quakerism, 18, 19, 42, 43, 53
Gustafson, J.M., 54

"hearing the light", 24
Hebrew and Christian tradition, 74
historic peace churches, 36
Holy Spirit, 24
Holy Spirit, doctrine of the, 8
Hopper, S.R., 32
House Church Movement, 60
Howgill, Francis, 77
humanitarian Quakerism, 78, 80

incarnation, 39
individual *versus* group, 26–28
individualism, 27, 28, 85
individualistic ethics, 68
inner light, 2, 8
institutional Christianity, 41, 44, 47, 51, 67, 75–76, 83
Iona Community, 60
irresponsibility, charge of, 34

Jesus Christ: and the Church, 57; centre of Quaker vision, 71; covenant of light, 9; covenant of Light, 18; foundation, 18; heavenly Prophet, 9; light of, 23–24; new way, 49; personal relationship with, 25; prophet, priest and king, 39, 44; resurrection of, 38; teacher of God's people, 9; teacher of righteousness, 23; truth, 28
Jones, Rufus, 46

Knox, John, 22
koinonia, 54, 56, 57, 64
Kraemer, Hendrik, 55, 65

laity, 60, 61, 64–65
Lamb's War, the, 47, 48
laos, 64
law and life, 16–18
Law of Moses, 16–17, 20, 37, 38
Lay Vocation, 64–65
liberal Quakerism, 3–5, 8

Index

liberty, 3, 26, 27, 28, 29, 30, 31
light and darkness, 14
Light of Christ, 24–25
light, inner. *See* inner light
Lippmann, Walter, 73
Loukes, Harold, 9
Lund Conference, 1952, v

mass man, 73
master–disciple relationship, 12, 18, 21, 37, 39, 44, *See also* dialogic relationship
Melchizedek, 11
Mennonites, 35
ministry and worship, 44
Modern Quaker Life, 77–78
moral perfectibility, 9
Mosaic Law. *See* Law of Moses
Mystery Babylon, 48
mystical Quakerism, 2–3, 6, 8, 78, 80
mystics, non-Christian, 3

Nachfolge. See obedience in ethics
nature of the church, 9
new covenant, 11, 25, 37–41, 49; religionless, 12
new covenant church, 65
new covenant community, 57
new testament as authority, 58
Nichols, James Hastings, 82
Niebuhr, Reinhold, 34, 35
Nietzsche, Friedrich W., 74
non-human world, 16
Norton, John, 50
Nottingham Conference 1964, 60
Nuttall, Geoffrey F., 7, 8

obedience, 24–25, 26, 27, 29, 30, *See also* corporate obedience
obedience in ethics, 33
Old and the New in the Church, The 54, 56
old covenant, 25
"orders" within the church, 36

Outler, Albert C., 53, 58, 59
"outsider", the, 72–77
Oxford Conference 1937, 62

"Parish Life Renewal", 60
Penington, Isaac, 10, 12, 13, 19, 22, 29, 44, 49–50, 70
Penn, William, 22
perfection, Quaker doctrine of, 23
Pietism, 5, 66–68
Pike, James, 84
Platonism, Christian. *See* Christian Platonism
pleading for sin, 22
"popery", 12–13
preaching, 42
Presbyterianism, 7
priesthood of all believers, 65
primary community, 83–84
professional ministry, 61–62
prophetic life, 16–18
prophetic Quakerism, 78, 80
prophetism, 69
Protestant church, 12–13, 83
Protestant ethics, 22
purgatory, 22
Puritan and Quaker, difference between, 9, 48–50
Puritanism, 7–8, 35, 49–50

Quaker ethics, 25
Quaker vision, 36, 70–72, 81
Quakerism, catholic (evangelical, humanitarian, liberal, modern, mystical, prophetic, quietist). *See* Catholic Quakerism, etc.
Quakerism, distinctive features, 5, 8–9
Quick, Oliver, 82
quietist Quakerism, 5

rebirth of the laity, 62
Reformation, 12, 35, 72, 82
renewal of the church, 41
revivalism, 5, 67

Index

righteousness, 15, 17, 20, 21, 24–25, 26, 27, 29, 30, 31, 33, 37, 39, 41, 47, 49, 70, 71, 75, 76, 84
Roman Catholic Church, 10, 12–13, 81
root and ground. *See* ground and root
Rowntree, John Wilhelm, 80
Russell, Elbert, 78

sacraments, 8, 9, 53, 55, 58, 59, 60, 66
salvation, 2, 15, 46, 67, 68, 84
science, 16
Scott, Richenda, 9
scriptures. *See* Bible
sectarianism, 77–78
shunning, 26, 31
sin, pleading for. *See* pleading for sin
"Solus Christus," *See* "Christ Alone"
state, relation to, 9
study groups, 63
style of life of Christian community, 33
suffering church, *See* church of the cross
suffering community, 83

Taylor, Thomas, 7
Tomkins, Oliver, 59
tradition, 57–60
tradition, Catholic and Protestant, 65
truth, 30
twentieth century man, 72–73

unity in Christ, 26, 27, 30, 53, 71
universalism, non-Christian, 3

victory of the Lamb, 47–48
vocational Christianity, 36

Welch, C, 7
Wesley, John, 5
we–thou relationship, 42 *See also* dialogic relationship
will of God, 29
Wood, H. G., 71
Woolman, John, 32
Worker Priests, 60
worship and ministry, 9, 13
Wright, G. Ernest, 75

Yoder, J.H., 33

www.ingramcontent.com/pod-product-compliance
Ingram Content Group UK Ltd.
Pitfield, Milton Keynes, MK11 3LW, UK
UKHW041419180426
11947UKWH00007B/218